EDUCATING
African American Males:
Detroit's Malcolm X Academy Solution

"The statistics are shocking! More than half of you Black men grow up to be ignorant in math ...that's almost 30%!"

Clifford Watson and Geneva Smitherman

E D U C A T I N G
AFRICAN AMERICAN MALES:
Detroit's Malcolm X Academy Solution

Progressive Black
Publishing Since 1967

Third World Press
Chicago

Students at Malcolm X Academy

About the Authors

Geneva Smitherman received her Ph.D. from the University of Michigan. Dr. Smitherman is University Distinguished Professor of English and Director of the African American Language and Literacy program at Michigan State University. Her published works include *Black Talk, Sounds of Soul, Talking and Testifying, Black English and the Education of Black Children and Youth, Ain't I A Woman: African American Women and Affirmative Action*, and *Reflections on Anita Hill-Clarence Thomas*.

Clifford Watson received his Ed.D. from Wayne State University. Dr. Watson developed the Male Academy concept for the Detroit Public Schools, which resulted in the establishment of six African-centered schools. He is the founder and Principal of the Malcolm X Academy in Detroit. His published works include *Afro American Pioneers in Science* and *Pride*, an educational handbook for teaching Black Studies.

This book is dedicated to our fathers, Robert Watson, and Harry Nelson Napoleon, the true heroes of the Black community.

Contents

Foreword

Malcolm X believed that education was key to Black people's development and empowerment. Readers of *The Autobiography of Malcolm X* will recall his struggle to master the words in the dictionary and how he worked his way from "A" to "Z." In this respect, Malcolm's philosophy was rooted in the tradition of Frederick Douglass and countless other Black leaders who tirelessly fought to achieve the twin goals of freedom and literacy for Africans in America. Malcolm's transformation from what today is known as "thug life" to Black Liberator and world leader serves as an educational inspiration to African American males and, indeed, is a reminder of human possibility everywhere.

The Malcolm X Academy in Detroit is an African-centered school which honors the legacy of Malcolm X in its commitment to the educational empowerment of Black males through self-knowledge and historical consciousness. I have visited the Academy, and I have talked with its teachers and its principal, and I have also given a presentation to Academy parents, teachers, and staff. I am impressed with the impact of the Malcolm X Academy on its Black male students, and I endorse the work that the Academy's staff and parents are doing. This book tells the story of that work.

Kwame Kenyatta, former Vice President,
and current member, Detroit School Board

Preface

I knew about Dr. Clifford Watson's work as a Detroit educator long before we became professional colleagues and comrades in educational struggle. I first heard about his work in the 1970's when I was teaching in African American Studies at Harvard University. At the time, I was considering a return to Detroit to work at Wayne State University's Center for Black Studies. As a teacher, community activist, and member of Detroit's Shrine of the Black Madonna, "Cliff," as he is known in the Detroit community, had gone against the odds and won the fight to establish Black Studies in a major inner city school district within the Detroit Public Schools. Actually, his target had been the entire Detroit Public School System, but "Region I" was an excellent launching site for the struggle. Those of us who were waging our own battles around institutionalizing African American Studies in the universities had come to realize that the Black Studies Movement had to reach out beyond the college level. Thus the few public school educators around the country—and they were few in that era—who, like Cliff, were putting their jobs on the line, had a special standing among Black Studies academicians like myself.

In the early 1980's, some years after Cliff's Black Studies battle, his name was again on the community grapevine. In those years, he was a math and science teacher at Detroit's Rosa Parks and Pelham Middle Schools. A pioneer in the Black all-male schools movement, Cliff had been fully cognizant of the educational onslaught against Black boys for much of his teaching career, but particularly since the late 1970's. While at Rosa Parks, a fourth- through sixth-grade school, Cliff organized an after school academic and athletic program for boys. In 1980, he labored over the plight of what sociologists and educators would come to label the "endangered species":

So many young Black males are on their way to being part of society's negative statistics. If school—or somebody—doesn't intervene on the elementary level, by the time these young Brothers are high school age, it'll be too late. By the teen years, they will have been suspended from school—forced out—on drugs, into street life and criminal activities, and on their way to jail, or an appointment with death. I can see it coming as young as third or fourth grade.

For some educators and scholars, the early 1980's marked the pivotal point where the reality of the Black male crisis could no longer be ignored. It was becoming painfully clear that young Black males experience negative social and educational problems, which have reached gigantic proportions today as we make our way to the Twenty-First Century. They were dropping out of school at alarming rates, and they were facing high rates of unemployment and incarceration. At the time, there were a number of programs designed for potential drop-outs, but hardly anyone was paying attention to the fact that the characteristics that made a student a "potential drop-out" were exhibited by African American males *as early as the third grade*: poor reading ability, discipline problems, low self-esteem. Many otherwise thoughtful people had begun to question whether these young Brothers could be rescued.

When Watson became Principal of Detroit's Peck Elementary School, he responded to the developing Black

male crisis by establishing the nation's first elementary
school drop-out prevention program, the precursor of
Detroit's male academy. Cliff remembers it this way:

> I designed the Peck Elementary School
> Drop-out Prevention Program to help young
> Brothers like Clifford, my namesake, whom I
> met at Peck back in the 1980's. The Program
> started with some of my friends who
> volunteered to be mentors. About twenty male
> students came to our first Saturday session. The
> incentive for them was basketball, but the
> requirement was that they had to spend at least
> one hour with a mentor in reading or math
> instruction to participate in the basketball
> program. It didn't take long for the word to get
> out in the community, and soon we had over 100
> students wanting to get into "Saturday School."
> As a result of this interest, I wrote a proposal to
> fund the expansion of the program, and several
> businesses adopted our Saturday School.

Skeptics often ask inner-city educators—those
struggling souls in the 'hoods of this nation—if they think
there is any hope for Black males. As a veteran in the
educational vineyards, Cliff doesn't just *think* it, he *knows* it.
Today in 1996, he has been witnessing the success of his
various educational programs for Black males for over a
decade. In particular, he likes to talk about his namesake
and where he is today:

> In over twenty years as an educator, I have
> had contact with thousands of students. But like
> most teachers, there are always a few who stand
> out. One of these was Clifford, my namesake,
> who, as I said, I had met at Detroit's Peck

Elementary School back in the 1980's. I was Peck's Principal at the time, and Clifford was a second grader who had been tagged as having "emotional problems" and labeled "learning disabled." It seemed like every other day Clifford was in my office because he had either been in a fight or had caused a disturbance in one of his classes.

Clifford fit the profile of the young Brother whose life is the "usual bleak story," as James Baldwin might have said. Both his parents were drug addicts, and he had been recruited by gang members to sell drugs. He lived with his grandmother, who was very concerned but who had little control over him. He was well on his way to becoming a "menace to society."

One of the businessmen who adopted our Saturday School was Mr. Dave Berry, whom I'll never forget. He developed a special interest in Clifford and took my namesake under his wing.

Mr. Berry was President of the Magni Corporation, an international paint company. He was a very unusual man. First of all, he was white! He took a special interest in our inner-city school and became a major financial contributor to Saturday School. Each year, Mr. Berry would invite the entire school out to his plush home in the suburbs for a picnic and swim in his Olympic-sized pool. There was always lots of food and prizes for the boys. He and his family seemed to enjoy all those little smiling Black faces. I couldn't help wondering what his white neighbors thought.

Like I said, Mr. Berry was an unusual man. He would take Clifford to lunch and started having him spend weekends at his big

> home out in the suburbs. Slowly, Clifford began
> a major metamorphosis: his grades and
> citizenship improved, and he was taken out of
> special education.
>
> Today, my namesake is a senior in high
> school doing above average work and looking
> forward to a career in the military.

The Peck Elementary School Dropout Prevention Program, which Watson had established back in 1984 to rescue at-risk Black males, eventually expanded from its base of reading and math to include foreign languages, computer science, and journalism. In 1985, it received national recognition in the *National Drop-Out Prevention Magazine* as well as many accolades from local and regional media throughout the 1985-86 school year. The Peck School Program, combined with conceptions of earlier male-centered educational programs created by Cliff, became the basis upon which the Detroit Public Schools established its three African-Centered Male Academies in the fall of 1991. Dr. Clifford Watson's educational vision for the education of African American males is evolving, and is now in its second decade.

My concern about the education of Black male students developed from my involvement in the *King* ("Black English") Federal Court case. Shortly after assuming the leadership of Wayne State University's Center for Black Studies in 1977, I began working with the parents and lawyers of a group of Black elementary school children who had taken the Ann Arbor School District to court, in the case of *Martin Luther King Jr. Elementary School Children vs. Ann Arbor District Board.* Residents of a housing project in Ann Arbor, Michigan, these young children had been victimized by that school district, which used the children's speech—Black English—as an excuse not to educate them, and to throw them upon the educational ash heap of the "learning disabled." In preparation for the month-long trial, which ended in a victory for us on July 12, 1979, I had organized a national group of linguists and educators to testify on the children's behalf. In February, 1980, I convened a national conference around the case. Yet, it was not until I heard Dr. Reginald Wilson (then President of Wayne County Community College, now Senior Scholar at the American Council on Education) cite statistics on the condition of Black males that a profound fact about that Ann Arbor group of children dawned on me: it was almost all male!

In the Introduction to *Black English and the Education of Black Children and Youth*, my 1981 book on the conference proceedings (in which Wilson's speech also appears), I wrote:

> If we are..."losing a generation," the schools should refuse to take part in this complicity....They can...save the children....Dr. Wilson's data....indicate that it may be Black males who are most desperately in need of saving....They rank highest among school dropouts, in crime statistics, in incarceration rates, in unemployment—and in being consistent speakers of Black English. In the schools, it is Black males who, disproportionately, comprise the "slow" reading groups....Among the plaintiff children, significantly, there were nine boys and two girls. There is a high degree of probability that these beautiful little dudes will grow up to take their place among the devastating statistics on Black males. I am not subscribing here to the mythical "privileged"

position of Black women nonsense—all the statistics show that to be a blatant falsehood. Rather, I am suggesting that progressive people must be clear about who the victims are—and who the enemy is. It [the enemy] is certainly not Black men, for these are our sons, our brothers, our fathers, and indeed, our lovers.

In 1988, as members of the Search Committee for the Chair of Wayne State University's newly-created Africana Studies Department, Cliff and I began a collaboration that culminated in the establishment of Detroit's Male Academies, which, in turn, led to this book. There remains much, much more work to be done in these educational vineyards. Here, at least, is a beginning.

Chapter One

SETTING AFOOT A NEW MAN

For Europe, for ourselves, and for humanity, comrades, we must turn over a new leaf, we must work out concepts, and try to set afoot a new man.
—Frantz Fanon, *The Wretched of the Earth*, 1963.

Although the deteriorating status of Black American males has become an issue of national focus in the 1990's, plans for their destruction have been a long time in the making. During the seventeenth century, when Europeans were preoccupied with ravaging the land that would become the United States, they lived in constant fear of Indian and African males. Historian Rhett S. Jones writes:

> The colonists and their American-born children knew, of course, that Native American women could and did fight against the invasion of their lands and that enslaved Black women often resisted. But...men were expected to be the primary warriors, and it was therefore Red and Black men whom White men feared (Jones, 1993, 3).

In the case of Black males, the Europeans' fear was not only related to the possibility of physical and violent resistance against them, but also to the economic threat posed by Black men who deployed their West African entrepreneurial skills throughout Britain's North American colonies. "Black men, drawing on West African traditions and shrewdly utilizing the insights they developed into the evolving European American culture, aggressively challenged White male hegemony" (Jones, 1993, 7). In the seventeenth and eighteenth centuries, this challenge came in the form of lawsuits and legal petitions against slavery (Quarles, 1973), rebellions, escapes from plantations, and use of the European Americans' rhetoric of "liberty and justice for all" as weapons against them (Bennett, 1969).

White males' perceptions of Black women, as well as the day-to-day lives of these women outside the Black world, were predetermined by the patriarchal society beginning to take root in the so-called "New World." In the early years of enslavement, African female slaves were assigned traditional women's work—domestic and housewifery duties—while male slaves were given field labor. Given the need for field hands and the European's notion that women could not do such hard labor, African males were more desirable than females as far as these early European Americans were concerned. The Tidewater planters, for instance, bought only male slaves in the first part of the eighteenth century (Gundersen, 1986). Naturally, the emphasis on the importation of African male slaves led to the shortage of Black women in the seventeenth and eighteenth centuries (Shammas, 1985), which is an ironic reversal of the sex-ratio imbalance today. This brings to mind the solution to the "problem of the Negro" posed by what Horace Mann Bond calls "one disturbed person," namely, to anually export fifty thousand Black women of child-bearing age, for a period of twenty years! The proponent of this plan even estimated the number of ships required, and the cost per capita to the federal government (Bond, 1934).

While African female slaves, in the seventeenth and

2

eighteenth centuries, were assigned domestic chores and other work that limited their mobility, Black male slaves had greater freedom to move about. Thus, they not only came into more frequent contact with other Africans, but with various groups of Whites as well.

> White hate for Black men is deeply rooted in European American culture...Black men represented a double threat to White men. As White males saw it, they were challenging White men in the White social order, while at the same time ruling a separate Black social order of their own. Blinded by their gender assumptions, eighteenth-century White men were unable to see that Black men and Black women shared rule of a social order they had created together, despite slavery and racism. Ignorant of the important role played by Black women in their culture, White males reserved a special animosity for Black men (Bond, 1993, 13).

Reflecting on his experiences as a young Black male in 1944, Judge A. Leon Higginbotham, Jr. paints an appalling picture of this "special animosity" at one of America's most prestigious universities. At the time, he was one of only twelve Black students at Purdue University:

> Solely because of our color [we] were forced to live in a crowded private house rather than, as did most of our white classmates, in the university campus dormitories. We slept barracks-style in an unheated attic.
> One night, as the temperature was close to zero, I felt that I could suffer the personal indignities and denigration no longer. The

Educating African American Males:
Detroit's Malcolm X Academy Solution

United States was more than two years into the
Second World War, a war our government had
promised would "make the world safe for
democracy." Surely, there was room enough in
the world...for twelve black students in a
northern university in the United States to be
given a small corner of the on-campus heated
dormitories for their quarters....I went to the
office of Edward Charles Elliott's office,
neatly...dressed, shoes polished, finger-nails
clean, hair cut short....I had not come that
morning to move mountains, only to get myself
and eleven friends out of the cold....Forcefully,
but nonetheless deferentially, I put forth my
modest request: that the black students of
Purdue be allowed to stay in some section of the
state-owned dormitories; segregated, if
necessary, but at least not humiliated
....President Elliott, with directness and no
apparent qualms, answered, "Higginbotham, the
law doesn't require us to let colored students in
the dorm, and you either accept things as they
are or leave the University immediately."

Almost like a mystical experience, a
thousand thoughts raced through my mind as I
walked across campus. I knew then...that one
day I would have to return to...this incident...a
legal system that proclaims "equal justice for
all" could simultaneously deny even a
semblance of dignity to a 16-year-old boy who
had committed no wrong (Huggingothan, 1978,
Preface).

There are those who argue that although the 1960's
produced some gains, since 1980, things have gotten worse
for African Americans, males in particular. Of course, one
could argue that the social condition of Black males has

always been deplorable, as our brief look at the history of Black males suggests. However, the social data have conventionally been reported in terms of simply Black and non-Black, without any separate attention to males compared to females. Only in the last five years has the alarming deterioration among African males in America been exhibited in social statistics. Sadly, these data indicated that this "endangered species" is at the bottom of every statistical indicator. Indeed, a 1984 study conducted by the Center for the Study of Social Policy, as reported in the Detroit Free Press in 1988, concluded that by the year 2000, more than 70% of Black men will be unemployed, jailed, addicted to drugs or alcohol, part of an underground economy, or otherwise out of the labor force indefinitely (Huskisson, 1988). In an update of its research on African American males, the Center for the Study of Social Policy reveals that the status of Black males has continued to decline in the ten years since its 1984 study:

> Almost four million out of the 9.8 million working-age black men...are without jobs...they are either unemployed, out of the labor force, in correctional facilities, or unaccounted for...the percent of working-age black men who are unemployed, discouraged workers, or unaccounted for is almost two times that for white men....If almost 40 percent of all black men are jobless—either unemployed, not looking for work, in correctional facilities or unaccounted for—it is little wonder that an increasing number of black women are raising families alone. (1993,7,9)

UNEMPLOYMENT

They keep on saying the Brothas don't
want to work. All I know is that Edison
[Detroit's electrical power company] had those
thirty jobs, and they just asked the people in that
section to tell a relative or friend who needed a
job. They weren't going to run an ad in the
paper or anything since they were only talking
about thirty measly jobs. Well, lo and behold on
that Monday, over 300 people showed up for
those pitiful little thirty jobs. —34 year old
Black male Detroiter in 1989 survey.

The figures below chart the unemployment rate for
males, Black and white, in the age group 16-19, from 1980
to 1992:

	1980	**1985**	**1992**
Black	37.5%	41.0%	42.0%
White	16.2%	16.5%	18.4%

(Source: For 1992, Center for the Study of Social Policy,
1993, p. 3; for 1980 and 1985, U.S. Department of Labor, pp. 139-
140.)

Bleak as these statistics are, they don't capture the full
unemployment situation because such data only include
males actively seeking work, receiving unemployment
benefits, or otherwise identified in official surveys. There
are thousands—perhaps millions—of other Black males
who don't show up in these statistics. They are part of the
huge group of people who constitute what labor economists
call the "hidden" unemployment rate. They are the

6

discouraged workers who are no longer looking, those who have never worked, and those who have never started looking for work in the first place because they know there are no jobs for them. The millions of people in this group—including the Black males in this number—don't show up in most official unemployment charts, nor in public agencies' computerized data bases. Further, since official statistics are based on U.S. Census data, we need to factor in the population undercount of Blacks. According to the Center for the Study of Social Policy, over 1 million Black males were not counted in the 1990 Census (1993, 3). In Correction for these omissions, Urban League data presents the following total unemployment rate for Black males, ages 16-19, from 1988 through 1993:

1988	1990	1993
55.6%	60.9	59.3%

(Source: National Urban League Research Department, Quarterly Economic Report on the African-American Worker, 1990, 1992, forthcoming.)

It is critical to remember that this unemployment pattern was not always so. In the 1930's and 40's, Black males, in the age group 14-20, were employed in great numbers in the trades and in the industrial plants. The corporations and industries of the nation needed Black males' labor, and Black males' families needed the income that this labor would bring into the household. The employment picture of the 1930's spawned an interesting irony. Since there were large numbers of teen-age Black males employed, especially in certain areas of the country, there were, of course, a smaller percentage of Black males in high school. However, their absence from school was often attributed to the lack of "ambition" and "push," an "explanation" that operated to the "detriment of the opinion in which the Negro boy [was] held by school administrators" (Bond, 1970, 221).

Today, the high rates of unemployment of African American males can be greatly accounted for by the de-industrialization of the U.S. economy which has taken place over the past two decades. Whereas African Americans, particularly males, could traditionally depend on being absorbed into the industrial and blue-collar work force, that option is no longer viable as America's industrial base declines and factories locate to parts of the world where wages are truly "minimum." Further, the new service jobs (save those at the "Mickey D's" of the nation, with their minimum-wage salaries) favor persons with technical skills and advanced education. The economic decline is so severe and the competition for what few jobs there are is so great that even a college education is no guarantee of employability—and, of course, racism still lingers like a cancer in the nation. For instance, Black males with a college degree are three times more likely to be unemployed than white males with comparable degrees. "Today, the unemployment gap between the college-educated Black man and the college-educated white man is actually higher than 10 years ago" (Senator Terry Sanford, 1991, 4).

INCARCERATION

In 1990, the National Sentencing Project announced its finding that "almost one in four (23%) Black men in the age group 20-29 is either in prison, jail, on probation, or parole on any given day" (Mauer, 1990, 3). Yet, this situation had

8

been evident for a number of years before the study results were released. In 1984, Black men were 37% of the prison population (Horton and Smith, 1990, 72). According to political scientist Charles P. Henry, by the late 1980's, Black men comprised half the male population in local, state and federal prisons, but they were only 6% of the U.S. population. These rates of Black male incarceration exceed those of South Africa, with all its apartheid and severe political oppression of Blacks. There, the rate of imprisonment for Black males was 729 per 100,000 compared to 3,109 per 100,000 in the United States. That was in the Sentencing Project's 1991 report. By the time it released its 1992 report, the rate had *decreased* in South Africa and *increased* in the U.S.: 681 per 100,000 in South Africa compared to 3,370 per 100,000 in this country (Mauer, 1991, 3; 1992, 1). Stated another way: "The United States imprisons Black males at a rate almost five times higher than South Africa" (Sklar, 1993, 60).

HOMICIDE

I still have nightmares about that day back in 1974 when my son, Tony, my brother, Benny, and Kutzie, my brother's best friend since first grade, were robbed at gunpoint. Other than my other brother, Hilton, and my father, these three young Black males were the most important men in my life. Every time I think about it, I get chills because I could have lost all three of them in one fatal stroke. Ted, the young Black male who robbed them, was a homeboy that Benny and Kutzie had gone to elementary school with. Ted's family, like mine, still lived in the hood, and although Ted didn't hang with them anymore, they saw him frequently in and about

9

the hood and always stopped to talk.

On this cold winter day, the men in my life were just chillin in my father's car, with Benny at the wheel. He had recently gotten his driver's license and was strutting his stuff to his boy, Kutzie, and his young nephew, Tony. They also were sporting the new coats they had gotten as Christmas gifts. Ted flagged the car down a couple of blocks from our house. Since no traffic was about, Benny stopped the car in the middle of the street, and they exchanged five's and "What up, doe's?" with Ted, a homeboy that Benny and Kutzie had played baseball with way back in little league days. Suddenly, out of nowhere, Ted pulled a gun and told them to "check it in." My son, my brother, and my brother's best friend surrendered their coats. Ted ran off. That was in 1974. Today in 1994, under similar circumstances, the men in my life would undoubtedly be killed.

—Geneva Smitherman,
Memoirs of a Daughter in the Hood.

Equally as bleak as the prison statistics are homicide rates for Black males. Homicide is the leading cause of death among African American males in the age group 15-24, and a Black male is twice as likely to die before the age of 45 as a white male (Detroit City Council, 1991, 4). As with other devastating statistics, the Black male homicide rate has always exceeded that of white males. The table below gives the overall Black male homicide rate in comparison to the white male rate over a thirty-year span.

HOMICIDE RATES—BLACK AND WHITE MALES, 1960-1989

	1960	1989
	(Rate over 100,000)	
Black	36.6	61.1
White	3.8	8.2

(Source: Bureau of Justice Statistics)

While the overall rate of death by homicide is certainly great, it becomes even greater if we consider only those Black males in the age group 15-24: 46.4 per 100,000 in 1960, and 101.8 per 100,000 in 1988 (Sklar, 1993, 57). Speaking to this horrifying state of affairs in the Black community, Gibbs notes that "in 1977, more young Black men (5,734) died from homicide than were killed from 1963-1972 in the Viet Nam War (5,640)" (1988, 258). In a series of articles on "Black Children in Trouble" in Essence Magazine, Weathers (1993) indicated that "guns are the number-one killer of [Black] teenagers....[M]ost young victims are males. Each day in America, guns kill an average of four Black male children under age 19" (Weathers, 1993, 70). These statistics don't begin to capture the hundreds of males who escape death by homicide only to be permanently crippled or otherwise seriously injured by gunshot wounds—a tragic condition these males will carry with them for life.

EDUCATION

In 1988, 40% of adult Black males were functionally illiterate (Detroit City Council, 1991, 19). In 1992, the Black male high school drop-out rate was estimated to be as

11

high as 60% in some urban areas. As has been pointed out by some scholars, the rate of Black males leaving high school is not significantly different from what it was in the past. However, the critical difference is that today, with the advent of high technology and the de-industrialization of America, there is no high-paying blue collar job market to absorb these young Black males. Before leaving school permanently, many of these males are likely to have been suspended and expelled, all at a higher rate than any other group, a tragedy that has led many educators to use the term "force-out" instead of "drop-out."

Even if Black males do stay in school, their educational success is not guaranteed. Typically, they lag behind Black females and whites. For example, they tend to be two or more grades behind normal, to a far greater extent than is the case for other race-sex groups, as can be seen from the following table:

PERCENT OF STUDENTS TWO OR MORE GRADES BEHIND IN SCHOOL BY RACE AND GENDER

Age	BMale	BFemale	WMale	WFemale
10-13	10.3	5.9	4.2	3.0
14-15	13.1	8.9	6.9	3.7
16-17	16.0	7.9	7.2	3.9
18-19	16.5	7.9	5.5	3.9

(Adapted from Center for the Study of Social Policy, 1993(a), p. 19).

Further, even though Black males stay in school, they tend to fall behind other race-sex groups in reading and math. Analysis of twelfth-grade data from the 1990 National Assessment of Educational Progress (NAEP) reveals this deplorable fact. In reading assessment, at what NAEP labels a "Level 300," which is a medium level only, note the following:

PERCENT OF 12TH GRADE STUDENTS AT READING ASSESSMENT LEVEL 300

BMale	BFemale	WMale	WFemale
12.2	17.2	40.5	48.8

(National Assessment of Educational Progress, 1990, as reported by Center for the Study of Social Policy, 1993, p. 20).

Black male performance on 12th-grade math assessment, again at the medium level, "Level 300," yields a similar comparison:

PERCENT OF 12TH GRADE STUDENTS AT MATH ASSESSMENT LEVEL 300

BMale	BFemale	WMale	WFemale
19.5	12.7	53.9	50.4

(National Assessment of Educational Progress, 1990, as reported by Center for the Study of Social Policy, 1993, p. 20)

These discrepancies in academic achievement, combined with the Black male high school force-out rate, help us to understand, in part at least, the low number of Black males in college. (Homicide, unemployment rates, and incarceration also take their toll on this aspect of Black male reality). From 1976 to 1986, the proportion of Black men attending college suffered the largest decline of all racial and gender groups (American Council on Education, 1988). Specifically, the rate of Black males enrolled in college in 1976 was 4.3 percent; by 1986, it had declined to

3.5 percent. By contrast, the rate of Black female college enrollment remained fairly steady over the same time frame, 5.1 percent in 1976, and 5.2 percent in 1986 (American Council on Education, 1988). Thus, for example, in 1991, there were only two Black males for every three Black females on U.S. college campuses (Detroit City Council, 1991, 20).

We could go on and on citing more deplorable statistics, but the situation is starkly clear. The status of African American males has hit rock bottom. We must set afoot a new man.

Chapter Two

NOBODY KNOWS MY NAME: BROTHERS BEHIND THE STATISTICS

I was born the fifth child of a nineteen-year old, unwed mother who had her first child at age 13. My father was a nineteen-year old who used heroin, was an alcoholic, and had three sons by two women in an 18-month period of time...my five brothers and I raised ourselves....Poverty was our mother, and the streets were our father. Motivation to complete school and plan our futures was rare, appeared insincere, and/or was not provided in a way or by a person with whom we would relate....

Today, my oldest brother, who is 30, has spent more than half his life in and out of...correctional facilities....My brother, 29, has been an alcoholic and user of crack cocaine for the last seven years and is currently in jail in Louisiana. My brother, 27, has at least five children by four women in three different states (that I know of). My brother, who is the only one by my mother and my father, is 25 and lives in Arizona, has had no legal address and no phone for the last two years, and has been in trouble with the law in Arizona for assault and for carrying a concealed weapon. My brother by my father, who is also 25, lives in Detroit, has no real job, and no desire to get one. He is currently on probation for possession of narcotics.

While growing up...I was no angel. I was involved in a number of fights and kicked out of school more times than I can remember. I have been shot at and shot, stabbed, sliced, and beat (once with a pipe). Somehow or other, I have never been arrested though I have been harassed by the police on numerous occasions...After the mistake of joining the Marine Corps (from which I was medically discharged), I went through a transformation during the summer of 1989...[when] I had a summer job...mentoring and tutoring kids from ten to fifteen years of age, who were first-time criminal offenders. They were my brothers and me all over again. It was a little late in my life, but I started to do some long-term planning....

I am now 24, married, with two children by my wife, and one child by sperm donation to a lesbian friend (with my wife's consent). I am currently working on my Ph.D. In retrospect, I see my brothers and myself as having had the same "opportunities" and the same potential for "success"...with the right guidance and cultivation, who knows where we could all be today?

—Kwame Johnson 1994.

⟪ℚ⟫

Two years ago, Leah Hasty, principal of Baltimore's all-Black Matthew A. Henson Elementary School in a neighborhood of housing projects, grassless yards and drug dealing, quietly created a second-and-third class for Black boys taught by a Black man, Richard Boynton....George Adams, 8, entered Boynton's class 2 years ago, shortly after he'd seen his older brother killed by a male baby sitter. His mother, Dornita Harris, a single parent on public assistance, was looking for stability and a positive male influence for George. "He needed that male behind him because he was starting to fall," Harris says.

Ask George about his teacher, and he grins. He talks

16

about his skills in math and reading he has learned, the Saturday field trips, how much he likes his teacher. But perhaps most telling is when he says simply, "I don't know many men like Mr. Boynton."

For George's mother, that is precisely the point of the class. "If being with Mr. Boynton can help George see what he can become if he works hard, gets an education and stays straight, that's all I ask....I don't know if I'll make it, but my kids have to."

—Nelson, 1991.

《◎

I was born Arthur Lee Hamilton, Jr., October 1957....the drama of my life of crime was played out in the theater of the city of Detroit....My entrance had been ill-timed and ill-placed into Detroit's recession-gripped ghettos, and into a family torn apart by abuse and alcoholism. Detroit's decline was intertwined with the fortunes of hundreds of thousands of people who were mostly Black....Before I ever thought of pulling a gun, circumstances and forces were coming into play in Detroit that made my criminal career and that of many other Black men almost inevitable....By the mid '60's, jobs and white people were leaving Detroit in droves....The loss of population and tax revenue was devastating for Detroit. Services shrunk, and of course for us they all but disappeared. In schools, class size grew as attendance plummeted....I said that poverty alone would not send people into a life of crime. But the poverty of spirit and mind, as well as that of the pocketbook (such as we encountered in the midst of the decline of Detroit) can

17

indeed set a person on a path to self-destruction.

...[T]he sentences of twenty-five to fifty years and twelve to fifteen for armed robbery and manslaughter added up to one long death sentence....I thought about the bums, drunkards, murderers, rapists, and all other nobodies who have died, and are buried in prison/pauper graves where weeds grow tall and dense, obscuring any sign of their previous existence. And then I thought about the kind of final resting place where loved ones come to place flowers on the graves and talk softly about what those below have left behind. A nice place, a quiet place where people are not ashamed to visit...[F]rom those two visions grew a desire, a reason, a purpose. I was determined not to leave prison a nobody, buried in a forgotten corner of some forgotten graveyard. I began to take advantage of the many positive programs that the Michigan prison system had to offer—to throw a few switches, to shed some light on my stage. One achievement led to another, and before I knew it, I began to feel like somebody—man, a father, a husband, a human being.

—Father Behind Bars, 1993

(Q

Looking back, I don't know why they didn't kill me before I became a teenager...actually my father almost did. And if he had, they would've called it justifiable homicide.

I really don't know why I was such a bad kid...I was always trying to get attention and so I acted like a juvenile delinquent. I never killed anyone or did drugs or anything like that, but I was bad...I'd beat people up, hit teachers, spit on people, break into cars and take tapes. I was a real jerk but I thought I was cool. In fact, my nickname...was

18

J.C.—Just Cool...

One of the things my father used to do was walk up to school unannounced to see what I was up to. You could call this "sneaking around," but my father, being an army dude, would call it "a reconnaissance mission." Anyway, on one of those missions he peered in a window and happened to see me strutting around, my shirt unbuttoned, showing off this big necklace I was wearing, actin just like a big goof. And he wailed me right there....

My father's lessons were simple: work hard, concentrate, be mentally tough, be persistent...my mother didn't like weakness either. Early on in Jersey City, back when I was the beaten instead of the beater, I would run in the house crying after a kid had picked on me, and my mother would say, "You truck right on back there and take care of business."

...See, my parents weren't the kind of people to just discipline me for no reason. They went after me when I was bad, but they praised me when I did good.

A little later, when I was in high school, I remember I was on a search for role models—Michael Jordan, Magic Johnson, people like that. Then I hit upon it one day that I really didn't have to look that far. My parents were my role models. All I had to do was pattern myself after them.

I'm glad my dad whupped me into line. When he has a problem at home now, with either of my younger sisters...or my brother...he gets me on the phone and I have to talk to them. I always say to my dad: "Bro, you're getting soft." Thank God he wasn't soft when I was growing up.

—Shaquile ("Shaq") O'Neal, 1993

19

*We call John King "The Comeback King." He has
seen some terrible days since entering the Malcolm X
Academy. His first year here ended with over four pages of
anti-social actions against the school, teachers, and
students. The turn-around for him began the day we talked
about "fear" and discussed how most people act up because
they are motivated by fear. John blurted right out in class,
"I'm scared, Miss Strong." Then the entire class began to
raise questions about why they are full of fear. This led to
several days of discussing fear, its causes, its consequences,
and the cure for it. The students used their journals to write
about nightmares and other fearful occurrences in their
lives. Since this time, John's behavior has changed
drastically. Of course, he still has problems, but nothing
compared to last year. We can witness the anger and fear
subsiding, his grades are improving, and he is now getting
along with other students and his teacher.*
—Malcolm X Academy Teacher

༄

*...The mind is like the body. If you don't work actively
to protect its health, you can lose it, especially if you're a
black man, nineteen years old and wondering, as I was, if
you were born into the wrong world.*
*...[T]hings were falling apart in my head much faster
than they were coming together. And I wasn't alone. I saw
it happening to most of the fellas around me: Greg, Shane,
Cooder, my older brother Dwight. We were bouncing
around like pinballs in a machine, wondering if the world
was fucked up or if we were: wondering why we were being
pushed into the backseat of life and couldn't get at the*

20

*wheel. If you're the only person riding in a car, and you're
not driving, there's nothing to do but crash.*
—Nathan McCall, *Makes Me Wanna Holler*, 1994

ᘚ

*Eighteenth Street was just one street out of many that
fell under our jurisdiction. The mechanics involved in
taking a street, or territory, is not unlike any attempt, I
would assume, on behalf of early Euro-American settlers.
Send in a scout, have him meet the "natives," test their
hostility level, military capabilities, needs, likes, and
dislikes. Once a military presence is established, in come
the "citizens"—in this case, gang members. Those who are
not persuaded by our lofty presence will be persuaded by
our military might. All who are of fighting age become
conscripts. The set expands, and so does our territory.
Sometimes there is resistance, but most of the time our
efforts are successful...This was my career, my "calling," as
church folks say when someone does one thing real well...*

*As of late, sets—which are the equivalent of a company
of military jargon—have started to use individual colors,
outside of the universally worn red and blue, to denote their
particular chapters...With each new generation of...bangers
comes a more complex system, which is now reaching
institutional proportions. It is precisely because of this type
of participation in the development and expansion of these
groups' morals, customs, and philosophies that
gangbanging will never be stopped from without...*

*...[Banging] did and still does supply wayward youth
with an idea of collective being and responsibility...It is,
unfortunately, the extreme expression of hopelessness in
New African communities: misdirected rage in the form*

21

of retarded resistance...

After having spent thirteen years of my young life inside what had initially seemed like an extended family but had turned into a war machine, I was tired and disgusted with its insatiable appetite for destruction...I wanted to construct something, which in banging is tantamount to treason.

It took me a full three years to get out of the Crips.
—Sanyika Shakur (A.K.A. Monster Kody Scott), 1993.

෴

Michael Green is a small-built young man who started at Malcolm X Academy in the fifth grade. Feeling his developing manhood, he was beginning to sound like a loud-mouth, a smart alec, who poked fun at other students when they made mistakes and who acted out in class. His mother had to be called to Malcolm X for conferences about Michael's disruptive behavior. She pledged cooperation, as did Michael. But saying and doing can be two different things. So I waited to see if he would clean up his act after being in the Malcolm X environment for a while. Sure enough, by the end of the semester, Michael was producing "B" level work, developing personal discipline, sharpening his musical ability. He is becoming a prime example of the Malcolm X Academy man.
—Malcolm X Academy Teacher

Chapter Three

IT TAKES A WHOLE VILLAGE TO RAISE A CHILD

In the last five years, several school systems and universities have finally begun to address the severe crises affecting African American males by establishing educational programs for Black males. One can only hope that the momentum will pick up before the crises begins to consume the national Black community. As of this writing in mid-1994, there are some thirty programs especially designed for African American males. Some of the programs are school-based; others are merely school-linked. Some programs involve all-male classes within a school; some are "pull-out" programs for selected males within a class; still others are after-school and/or Saturday programs. Hopkins (1994, 40) categorized the programs into five types: 1) whole male schools; 2) evolving (whole) male schools; 3) single-gender classes; 4) school-affiliated programs; and 5) community-based programs. We shall follow his categorizations in describing Black male educational programs across the country.

DETROIT AND "WHOLE MALE SCHOOLS"

The Detroit Public School District is the national model for Black all-male public schools, as it was the first district to experiment with such an approach. As a result of a year-long study by the Superintendent's Task Force on the

Male Academy (Detroit Public Schools, 1991), on which both Watson and Smitherman served, three all-male elementary schools were established in Detroit, in 1991: Malcolm X, Marcus Garvey, and Paul Robeson. The program for these Academies was based on Watson's educational concept, dating back to the 1980's and his tenure as an administrator at Detroit's Pelham and Peck Elementary Schools.

Detroit's student population remains overwhelmingly African American; in 1990, it was only 2% white. Thus, the question of race did not present an issue in the establishment of the three male academies. However, gender did—at least for some segments of the greater metropolitan community. Thus a federal court battle delayed the implementation of the Male Academy Task Force's recommendation and the opening of these schools in September, 1991. Responding to a legal brief filed by the American Civil Liberties Union and the National Organization of Women Legal Defense and Education Fund, Federal Judge George Woods ruled that Detroit's Male Academies constituted discrimination based on sex. The District's Male Academy educational concept was retitled "African-Centered," and the three "Male Academy" elementary schools finally opened in late fall, 1991. In the intervening years, three other African-Centered Academies have been established, which are female-oriented. Despite Judge Woods' ruling, today in 1994, the Detroit Public Schools' original "Male Academy" concept continues virtually in full force. All three of Detroit's first African-Centered Academies have annually had a student population that is 90% or more Black male. They are the result of the Black community's protest against what many Detroiters perceived as interference from people who do not live in the city and/or whose children do not attend the public schools in Detroit. (For a full discussion of the court

24

battle over the Male Academy, see Chapter Four).

MILWAUKEE AND "EVOLVING MALE SCHOOLS"

Although Detroit was the first public school district to actually establish Black all-male schools, it was in Milwaukee, Wisconsin that district-wide attention was first focused on the education of African American males. Milwaukee created a special commission to study the condition of Black male students in that city. The commission's work resulted in the formulation of a comprehensive proposal for Black all-male schools at the elementary school level (Milwaukee Public Schools, 1990). That proposal, however, was not to come to fruition because of mounting concern about, and developing resistance against, what was perceived as a program that would "resegregate" Milwaukee's students. Since its school population was only about 40% Black at the time, the Milwaukee Public School District withdrew its plan for establishing all-Black male schools, fearing impending legal action based on a claim of racial exclusion. Instead, Milwaukee developed two "African American Immersion" schools: Dr. Martin Luther King, Jr. and Robert L. Fulton Middle School (recently re-named "Malcolm X African American Immersion School"). Both schools enroll males and females and have some non-African students. The curriculum emphasizes African and African American history and culture. The schools are currently conducting research on strategies for educating Black males and females.

NEW YORK'S UJAMAA INSTITUTE/
AN "EVOLVING" MALE SCHOOL

Ujamaa Institute was designed as an experimental high school for African American and Latino males, to be operated under the dual auspices of the New York City Board of Education and Medgar Evers College in Brooklyn, New York. The concept for the Institute combines New York Board of Regents requirements with an African-centered curriculum. The Institute proposal was over four years old when it opened its doors in September, 1994. Its opening had been delayed by racism masquerading as bureaucracy (Mchawi, 1993).

BALTIMORE, WASHINGTON, AND MIAMI
SINGLE GENDER CLASSES

In Baltimore, Maryland, Washingon, D.C., and Miami, Florida, the decision was to opt for individual Black male classes within the school. This strategy was employed to avoid litigation over racial and/or gender "exclusion." Six such schools exist: Coldstream, Robert Coleman, George G. Kelson, and Matthew A. Henson Elementary in the Baltimore Public School District; and Pine Villa Elementary "at-risk male classes" in the Dade County District.

The Baltimore and Washington single gender classes were established in the 1989-90 school year. The classes are taught by African American male teachers and/or. Black male teacher assistants beginning in kindergarten and/or second grade. The class at Matthew A. Henson began in the second grade and was designed for students and teachers to stay together as the students were promoted. Interestingly enough, a conscious decision was made not to stress African-centered pedagogy or curriculum content in these

26

classes; according to Holland (1993), this was to avoid burdening these programs with yet another layer of controversy and conflict. He argues that the strategy of the Black male role model in the classroom will make the difference. The Teacher Assistants are trained in Holland's "Project 2000" program at Morgan State University in Baltimore. (See discussion of "Project 2000," page 31)

At Miami, Florida's Pine Villa Elementary School, there are two "at-risk male classes," serving Black males from female-headed families whose income is largely from federal and local welfare sources. There is a kindergarten and a first-grade class, both of which were implemented during the 1987-88 school year. As far as we were able to determine, the curriculum is not African-centered; the focus is on a mentoring kind of "buddy system," appropriate school behavior, and conflict resolution.

AFTER-SCHOOL, PARTNERSHIPS, AND SCHOOL-AFFILIATED PROGRAMS

There are (13) such programs in cities across the country; twelve are discussed here.

CLEVELAND-EAST END NEIGHBORHOOD HOUSE

This is an African-centered Rites-of-Passage program for males and females in the Cleveland, Ohio Public Schools. Involved are fifth and sixth-graders at Kirk Middle School. Students meet two afternoons a week, and Saturday mornings.

SAN DIEGO–FULTON ACADEMICS AND ATHLETIC MAGNET

Two components make up this program in San Diego, California: one for Black male students, the other for their teachers. A full-time African American male student advocate meets weekly with the school's Black males in classroom groupings. For the students, the program offers training in African and African American culture and history, individual and group counseling, and tutorial services, provided in conjunction with a volunteer network of African American males. For the teachers, there is staff development focusing on learning styles and issues pertinent to African American males.

SACRAMENTO—THE HAWK PROJECT

In the fall of 1988, the Hawk program was initiated by the Institute for the Advanced Study of Black Family Life and Culture of Oakland, California, in conjunction with Sacramento's Grant Union High School. The primary goal of the program is to develop male responsibility, particularly in regards to teenage pregnancy, drugs, gangs, and academic achievement. African and African American rituals are combined with lessons in history and culture for students who enroll in ninth grade and continue in the Hawk program until graduation. During the school day, students attend "pull-out" class sessions and there are two after-school classes each month.

RALEIGH—HELPING HANDS

In the Wake County Public School District, Raleigh, North Carolina, Black males in grades three through eight are matched with African American mentors, first from the school system, then from the community. Activities and strategies are targeted at four areas: self-esteem, school achievement, interpersonal relations, and leadership development.

MILWAUKEE—INROADS YOUTH LEADERS ACADEMY

This program for third through fifth grade Black males has been in operation in Milwaukee, Wisconsin since 1990. It was developed under the auspices of Inroads/Wisconsin, with after-school and Saturday classes on academics and personal skills, such as decision-making.

Volunteers from a variety of backgrounds and professions mentor students at Paul Robeson Academy in an after-school program that meets for two hours on Wednesdays. (Paul Robeson is one of the three African-centered male academies established by the superintendent's Male Academy Task Force). At the weekly sessions, community people also meet with the mentors in a kind of "think tank" forum to discuss issues of common concern.

DETROIT—MANHOOD INCORPORATED

Mentors in this program at the Marcus Garvey Academy are the male parents and caregivers of the students. This program seeks to expose its male students, especially those without males in the home, to male role models. (Garvey is one of the three African-centered male academies established in 1991). On Tuesday and Thursday afternoon, the parents/care givers meet with the students to provide mentoring and tutoring.

DETROIT—SAVE A STAR

A drop-out prevention program at Detroit's Monnier Elementary School, Save a Star was established in 1987 in response to the alarming number of male students in grades three through five who were being referred to the principal for disciplinary action, and who were being suspended from school. The program targets male students with below-average citizenship and academic grades to meet with a teacher, a social worker, and a counselor on a weekly basis. Several times each month, the students meet with male role models who have beaten the odds.

DETROIT—STARS

This is a mentoring program at Woodward Elementary School, founded by former Principal Dr. Clifford Watson, then Assistant Principal Ms. Judith Jackson, and kindergarten teacher Ms. Debra Walls. It currently serves African American male students in grades three through five, providing them with volunteer male mentors/tutors from Detroit's Black Men, Incorporated and from a local Detroit Armory.

EAST LANSING—"MY BROTHER'S KEEPER"

"My Brother's Keeper" Program of Michigan State University, East Lansing, Michigan, was established by Smitherman in 1990, utilizing educational outreach concepts developed by Watson. The Program matches African American students attending the University with elementary school-aged Black male students enrolled in the Detroit Public schools. (Although the program has operated at other Detroit elementary schools, currently, it is servicing only the Malcolm X Academy). The University students serve as mentors and role models, working with their Detroit students on Saturdays and during the summer. The goal is to introduce Black males early on to a college environment and inspire them to visualize a college education in their future.

TALLAHASSEE—BLACK MALE COLLEGE EXPLORERS

This program operates under the auspices of Florida A&M, the state's only public historically Black college. It targets Black male students in grades eight through twelve, focusing on preparing them for college by way of a six-week intervention program that the students attend each summer. For those students who stay with the program and achieve academically, entrance to the college of their choice is guaranteed.

ATLANTA—MOREHOUSE MENTORING PROGRAM

Operating under Morehouse College's Office of Community Service, this mentoring program is designed for pre-college Black males in Atlanta, Georgia. It seeks to promote the "Morehouse Tradition" through mentoring, community service, and tutoring.

BALTIMORE—PROJECT 2000

This program was established as the primary program under the Center for Educating African American Males at Morgan State University in Baltimore, Maryland. Under the leadership of psychologist Dr. Spencer Holland, Project

2000 recruits and trains Black males to serve as teacher assistants in several kindergarten through third grade classrooms, both those which are all male, as well as those which have boys and girls. Project 2000 operates in the Baltimore, Washington D.C. and Miami, Florida single-gender classes mentioned above; it operates in classes in the public school systems of Paterson, New Jersey; Kirkwood, Missouri; Newark, New Jersey; Annapolis, Maryland; and it operates in New Brunswick, New Jersey, where the teacher assistants are corporate employees given released time to participate in Project 2000. Finally, there is a Project 2000 in a private African American school in Chicago, Illinois.

COMMUNITY—BASED PROGRAMS

Following Hopkins (as discussed on page 23), we include in this category those programs designed by fraternities, churches, civic groups, and community organizations. The following are such programs known to us as of this writing.

CINCINNATI—RAAMUS

"RAAMUS" (Responsible African American Men United in Spirit) is located in Cincinnatti, Ohio and was founded by Dr. Kenneth Ghee in 1985. "RAAMUS" was an after-school program of education and "re-education" for males 9-14 years of age. The Program used the concept of "edutainment," a strategy employing entertainment and fun to educate young Black males about African American cultural heritage, and to motivate academic achievement.

TAMPA—CHILDREN OF THE SUN

Children of the Sun, a Washington, D.C.-based organization, joined hands with the Greater Tampa Urban League to create a 14-week after-school program for Black males from 10 to 18 years of age in Tampa, Florida. It is unique among Black male programs because it incorporates health as one of its primary foci, utilizing the services of an African American male physician to give presentations on health and disease prevention, and to provide physical examinations of the males in the program. A 14-week course reinforces health issues and also focuses on African American history and culture. There are also mentors and a "Rites of Passage" program.

WASHINGTON, D.C.—CONCERNED BLACK MEN, INC.

This is a mentoring program utilizing the Project 2000 concept. The students were third-grade Black males when the program was initiated in the 1990-91 school year. In addition to seminars on topics such as self-esteem, concerned Black Men sponsors a Martin Luther King Jr. Oratory Contest and an African American History Bee for students in the program.

BALTIMORE—PROJECT ALPHA

This mentoring program for Black males of all ages is sponsored by Alpha Phi Alpha, the oldest African American Greek-letter fraternity. Although headquartered in the fraternity's national office in Baltimore, there are nation-wide Project Alpha programs under the auspices of individual Alpha Phi Alpha chapters. Highlights of the program are seminars, workshops, and presentations on male responsibility, health awareness, and moral/religious issues.

NEW YORK—TOUSSAINT INSTITUTE FUND

This program makes a concerted effort to locate low-income, elementary school-aged Black males who are experiencing repeated failure in the public schools. The organization guarantees these males 90% of the funding necessary to attend a historically Black college.

Clearly, there is national support for special programs to educate Black male youth. The case of the overwhelming Black community mandate for Detroit's Male Academies is not unique to that city. Rather, Detroiters' sentiment parallels the strong national Black support for all-male public schools. In a 1993-94 survey of African Americans, 62% were in favor of the creation of such schools (Dawson, 1994). Commenting on the disbanding of successful Black male classes in Dade County, Florida (due to apprehension about a legal challenge), Holland argues:

> We cannot allow programs that show tremendous promise for the education of inner-city Black males to be eradicated without our vehement objections. The African American community must step forward and protest this type of bureaucratic insensitivity to the needs of our children. (Holland, 1991, 42)

The operative word here is "community," for indeed, it takes a whole village to raise a child.

Chapter Four

BY ANY MEANS NECESSARY: THE COMMUNITY STRUGGLE TO CREATE MALCOLM X ACADEMY

Like young African American male students throughout this country, Black males in the Detroit Public Schools are in a state of crisis. Without wholesale intervention, the deterioration will not only continue, it will get worse. In the last school year, 14,274 males were expelled from Detroit schools, double the number of females expelled (McGriff, 1993). In both of the last two school years (1991-93), more Detroit males, ages 15-19, graduated to the criminal justice system than graduated from Detroit high schools. Specifically, 2,244 teenage males graduated from high school in June, 1992, but 2,783 were charged in Detroit courts. In June of 1993, there were 2,200 15-19-year-old males on their way to receiving high school diplomas, but nearly 3,000 had been arrested and jailed (Detroit Free Press, 1993).

FIRST ANNUAL SAVING THE BLACK MALE CONFERENCE—MARCH, 1990.

Detroit was and is a community in crisis. It was this debilitating state of affairs in the schools that led an Ad Hoc Group of Concerned Educators to organize the first public school conference on the problems facing African American males. The Ad Hoc Group was spearheaded by Joseph Gilbert, Principal of Detroit's Mackenzie High School; Calvin McKinney, Principal of Detroit's Brooks Middle School; Smitherman, representing Michigan State University; and Watson, then Principal of Detroit's Woodward Elementary School. The Conference was entitled "Improving Self-Concept for At-Risk Black Students, with Emphasis on Saving the Black Male" (Detroit Public Schools, 1990). It was convened on Saturday morning, March, 10, 1990, a typical Michigan winter day of sub-zero temperatures and plenty of wind-chilling "Hawk." Being realistic, the Ad Hoc Group did not anticipate a large turn-out. They would have been happy with 100 people— at least that would have been a start. When the doors of Brooks Middle School opened on that cold Saturday morning in March, nearly 500 people were there, with standing room only—teachers, parents, seniors, and a few students. The Ad Hoc Group knew then that they were on the right track.

The Conference featured two keynote speakers who had both sounded the clarion call on the status of African American males: Dr. Jewelle Gibbs of the University of California-Berkeley, mother of two sons, and author of a 1988 book on Black males, and Mr. Haki Madhubuti, of the Institute of Positive Education, father, and author of a 1990 book on African American males. They challenged this large gathering of Detroiters to rethink and redefine their purpose in life and that of the community's Black youth—male and female. (See Appendix for excerpts from their Conference speeches.)

The Conference was conceived of as an action event, charging each participant to commit to a course of action, however small, to further the education and life-chances of Black males. They were asked to sign pledges, such as volunteering time to the school in their neighborhood, serving as mentors to students in need of role models, etc. Most importantly, the 500 people assembled there that wintry day unanimously passed a resolution, a "Charge to Elected Officials" in Detroit and the State of Michigan. The resolution was forwarded to the offices of the Governor, to all local and State elected political representatives, and to the Detroit Board of Education. The Conference Resolution called for these officials to convene hearings on the crisis of the African American male. (See Appendix for a copy for the Conference Resolution).

The Detroit School Board was moved by this symbolic gathering of citizens responding to the call and the crisis of the city's Black male youth. Three months after this first Detroit Public Schools "Saving the Black Male" Conference, the School Board, acknowledging the community's mandate, appointed a Male Academy Task Force to study the issues and bring to the Board a plan and implementation strategies.

MALE ACADEMY TASK FORCE

The Male Academy Task Force of eleven persons was deliberately kept small; it was comprised of educators in and outside the Detroit Public Schools, a county health executive, the Director of the Detroit Youth Home, and one elected official. Convened under former Detroit Superintendent Dr. John Porter, the Interim Deputy Superintendent, Dr. Arthur Carter, chaired the Task Force. The group consisted of four women, among them Dr. Geneva Smitherman and a female parent, and seven men, including Dr. Clifford Watson and Joseph Gilbert. Smitherman, Watson, and Gilbert had been part of the Ad Hoc Group that had organized the"Saving the Black Male"

37

March 1990 Conference that had spurred the School Board to action.

The deadline for the Male Academy Task Force's report to the School Board was November, 1990, only six months after it began its deliberations. Fortunately, though, the Task Force did not have to start from scratch since the group had the benefit of Watson's guiding proposal, as well as the benefit of his many years of experience with school-based programs for Black males. The Task Force submitted its report in December, 1990.

When they began their work, none of the Task Force members—save, perhaps, Watson—fully realized the extent of the deteriorating status for the city's Black male youth. As research, reports, and fact-finding proceeded, an oft-heard comment was "I knew it was bad, but I didn't know it was that bad!" The data amassed by the Task Force indicated that Detroit's Black male youth did indeed warrant the label "at-risk."

The overall male drop-out rate was 54%, and for those two years behind in grade level, the drop-out rate was 80%. Two-thirds of the school suspensions were male. Of the 24,000 males who were enrolled in Detroit Public Schools at the time, fewer than 30% had cumulative grade point averages above 2.0. Test data in fourth, seventh, and tenth grades indicated that a disproportionate number of males were under-achievers in reading and math. Of the graduates from Detroit high schools, only 39% were males (Detroit Public Schools, 1991, 6).

The Task Force found that the African American male unemployment, homicide, and crime statistics mirrored the bleak profile for males in the schools. At the time of the Task Force report in late 1990, Detroit's Black male unemployment rate was 18.3%, compared to 7.1% for the rest of the State, a figure that doesn't begin to account for the "hidden" unemployment rate—i.e., those males who have never worked, have stopped looking, or have been missed in the Census undercount. The homicide rate for Detroit males 18 and younger had accelerated from 54 per 100,000 in 1980 to 292 per 100,000 in 1987. In Wayne County, which includes Detroit and is the largest county in the State, the homicide rate for Black males, ages 15-24 was almost twice the rate for Black males in the entire state and 47 times the homicide rate for white males in Michigan. Of the 4100 youth admitted to the Wayne County Youth Home for juvenile offenses, 3500 were from Detroit. Sixty percent of the drug offenses in the county were committed by eighth and ninth grade drop-outs, and 97% of the offenders were African American males (Detroit Public Schools, 1991, 4).

Clear about who it was that needed "saving," the Task Force reached this conclusion about the target population to be served by Detroit's Male Academy:

> There are thousands of young males that can be characterized "at risk" because of difficulties associated with urban poverty and violence, family unemployment, single-mother households, lack of positive male role models, and lack of healthy, nurturing home environments. Some males are at-risk simply because they are negatively influenced by a peer group that is often more concerned about clothes, money, and social status than academics (Detroit Public Schools, 1991, 19).

Finally, Task Force research revealed that despite the controversy about male academies, educational systems all across the country are failing inner-city males (see, New Orleans Public Schools, 1988; Poinsett, 1988; Riordan, 1990; Soderman and Phillips, 1986). Thus, Detroit's Male

Academy Task Force was unanimous in its call for a Male Academy:

> A male academy was one of the most promising vehicles...to change the odds for "at-risk" male students...a male academy that is preventative in nature; utilizes multiple resources; and that marshalls the support of families, community members and role models, maximizes opportunities to focus on the unique needs of urban males at the kindergarten level through eighth grade (Detroit Public Schools, 1991, 8).

The Male Academy was conceived as a demonstration school. It was to be

> An experiment to determine if a restructured school, a redesigned curriculum and a comprehensive system of supports sensitive to the unique needs of males, can reverse the tide of failure among urban males and save a generation of children. If the Academy succeeds as expected, the District will seek to replicate the successful strategies and interventions at school sites all across the city (Detroit Public Schools, 1991, 9).

The Male Academy was to be open to all elementary-age students in the City of Detroit. Admission would be determined by lottery, with the critical exception that the process would be structured to reflect a heterogeneous population, reflecting varying degrees of risk or need: high, mid, and low. Seven variables identified as at-risk or need would be used in the selection of students: 1) citizenship; 2) days absent; 3) single parent status; 4) mother's highest grade of school completed; 5) grade point average; 6) number of times retained in grade; and 7) California Achievement Test reading percentile. Points were to be assigned to the students status for each variable, and the variables weighted, using the "At-Risk Variables Tabulation Scale" developed especially for the Male Academy. Once the sample was separated by grade level and stratified into three rankings of risk, one-third of the student population was to be randomly selected from each of the three categories of risk. The Male Academy Task Force thought it crucial to have this mix, given the strong influence of peers among males (Detroit Public Schools, 1991, 21).

Six primary principles were recommended to guide the mission, curriculum, and pedagogy of the Male Academy:

> 1) Afrocentric—Students learn about their own ethnicity...Multiculturalism extends across subject areas, shows connections, and relates the experiences of African Americans and others to present-day conditions.
> 2) Futuristic—Lessons stress 21st-century careers and jobs and highlights African Americans and others in these career fields...preparation and...training for high demand areas (engineers, computer technicians, robotics, etc.)
> 3) Linguistic—The power of communication is taught by developing oral, written, and foreign-language skills. Debate, forensics, public speaking...writing [are]...used to teach students to think critically, to solve problems and to resolve conflicts.
> 4) Civic—Emphasis...upon teaching

students to accept responsibility, first, for themselves...and then for bettering the conditions and/or relationships at home, school, and in the community.

5) Holistic—The curriculum relates to... the total person who has cognitive, aesthetic, spiritual and personal needs that must be addressed...strategies for meeting the unique needs of males especially in the areas of self-esteem and leadership.

6) Pragmatic—Students will learn practical, useful skills that promote self-confidence and a sense of accomplishment ...activities that involve building, creating, constructing....(Detroit Public Schools, 1991, 27-28).

The Male Academy was established as an "empowered" school within the Detroit Public School District. An "empowered" school is one that functions autonomously within the public school sector, but is still bound by the legal policies of the District and the State. Although it must operate within certain District parameters, it is free to design its own curriculum, determine its yearly calendar, select its own staff, and manage its own financial affairs (subject to Board oversight). As an empowered school, the Academy's mandate was to strive for the designation of "excellence," which would be based upon achievement of outcome goals articulated in Detroit's Quality Education Plan for the District:

Daily attendance that averages 95% or better; seventy-five percent of students scoring in the highest category on the Michigan Educational Assessment Program (MEAP) reading, mathematics and science tests; seventy-

five percent of students scoring at or above
grade level on the California Achievement Test
(CAT) of reading and mathematics; student code
violations at 5% or less; a non-promotion rate of
3% or less; and a grade point average of 2.5 or
above (Detroit Public Schools, 1989).

The Malcolm X Academy as Detroit's first Male
Academy was created early in 1991. By the summer of that
year, however, overwhelming demand for educational
programs for the sons of the Detroit community led to the
School Board's decision to create two additional Male
Academies: the Paul Robeson and the Marcus Garvey
Academies.

BIRTH OF THE MALCOLM X ACADEMY

The establishment of Detroit's first Male Academy was
fraught with controversy, beginning with its chosen name,
"Malcolm X." After submitting a preliminary report to the
Detroit School Board in December, 1990, the Male
Academy Task Force decided to give a name to the
Academy so as to avoid continued reference to it as the
"Male" Academy. Actually, early on, believing that there
would be possible legal problems for the District, Watson
had requested that the term "male" not be used, and he had,
in fact, petitioned then-Superintendent John Porter to name
the Academy "Malcolm X." However, Porter had rejected
Watson's request. In any case, the designation "Male
Academy" was beginning to cause quite a stir, most of it
emanating from the National Organization of Women
(NOW). This group, which is virtually all-white, contended
that the Detroit Public School System was returning to the
segregated school concept of pre-1954 (the year of the U.S.

Supreme Court ruling in *Brown vs. Board of Education*, which dismantled the legal segregation of schools in the South). Of course, racially segregated schools in the North, due to white flight out of the "Chocolate Cities" into the "Vanilla Suburbs," continued in full force after 1954. This explains why the Detroit Public Schools only have a 2% white student population—a situation that NOW opponents have never protested, even in the 1970's during the Detroit School Board's court fight in the case of Bradley v. Milliken. Bradley would have desegregated Detroit's schools by involving suburban districts. However, in 1974, the U.S. Supreme Court ruled against such a plan, thus setting a precedent that would be followed in other urban districts, which were also becoming racially segregated due to white flight.

The dire circumstances facing Detroit's Black male students and the fast-approaching deadline for the completion of its implementation report did not leave the Male Academy Task force much time to deliberate about the question of a name. From the outset, Superintendent Porter and other Black conservative forces in the administrative hierarchy of the District thought the name "Malcolm X Academy" was too "radical." Following a proposal from Smitherman, the Task Force settled on the name "David Walker," an ironic compromise. On the one hand, although it was not as well known as some other heroic names in Black history, it was a common name, not a "radical" one and thus should prove readily acceptable. On the other hand, David Walker was author of a revolutionary document, published in 1829, entitled "Appeal to the Coloured Citizens of the World, But in Particular, and Very Expressly, to Those of the United States of America." Walker's Appeal came from an unapologetic Afrocentric perspective and called for self-defense and armed struggle to

44

overthrow enslavement, views which probably caused
Walker his life. He was found dead near his shop on June
18, 1830, just months before the birth of his son.

The work of the Task Force, as well as those in the
educational hierarchy who disapproved of a Male Academy,
represented, after all, only the deliberations of a few. The
people themselves would speak on the name issue. Thus the
Male Academy Task Force's final report was delivered as
the report on the "Male Academy."

The Board members who had run in the previous
election as the "Hope Team"—Frank Hayden, Joe Blanding,
David Olmstead, and Lawrence Patrick—were key
supporters of the Male Academy proposal. Especially
critical was the support of Hayden, who was Board
President at the time, and without whom, the Task Force's
efforts—and Watson's long-awaited dream—would not have
become reality. History records that Board member Gloria
Cobbin cast the sole negative vote against the proposal.

In its acceptance of the report, the Detroit School
Board had ruled that the parents, teachers, and students
would have the right to name their school. The school-
community group that participated in the life of the first
Male Academy decided unanimously to call their school
"Malcolm X Academy." The name was chosen in
recognition of the "extraordinary series of personal
transformations...that brought [Malcolm] out of the
degradation of the street to a catalytic place" in African
American history (Logan and Winston, 1982, 422). Born on
May 19, 1925, in Omaha, Nebraska, attending school in
Lansing, Michigan, and hustling on the streets of Boston, he
progressed from Malcolm Little, school drop-out at 15,
convicted criminal at 21, to El-Hajj Malik El-Shabazz,
founder of the Organization for Afro-American Unity and

world leader of African people until his assassination on February 21, 1965. Malcolm was able to convey the most complex ideas with clarity and dramatic imagery, stressing re-education and self-knowledge in the quest for Black empowerment. The Malcolm X Academy family hoped that the legacy of Malcolm's "chronology of changes" would inspire its Black male students not only to transform themselves but also to position themselves as community and world leaders.

The Academy opened its doors in late September, 1991, on the first floor of an existing school, the Woodward Elementary School. Clifford Watson served as principal of both schools throughout school year 1991-92. It was to be an experimental school, whose staff would eventually be used to train educators at other schools on techniques for improving the performance of males in a co-educational setting. Male mentors and teachers would be used to establish role models for the Academy's male students. No female was to be denied admission although the curriculum and program would be male-centric. However, before the Academy was to get to its appointed task—the education of Detroit's young Black males—there would be a bitter court battle, marching, picketing, angry School Board meetings, and controversial local and national media coverage.

ATTACK FROM OUTSIDE THE COMMUNITY

We hadn't realized what Frederick Douglass really meant when he said, "Power concedes nothing." There truly cannot be progress without struggle.

On March 26, 1991, Superintendent John Porter received a letter from the National Organization of Women (NOW), addressing their concerns about the establishment of an academy for African American males. Subsequently,

Dr. Porter requested an expert opinion on the legal status of a "male" academy. Professor Robert A. Sedler, of Wayne State University's Law School, was retained as the Board's legal consultant. It was Sedler's opinion, as that of the Task Force, that the long list of problems facing Detroit's male students urgently demanded the creation of some alternative to Detroit's existing educational programs. These problems had been cited in the Task Force's report as the rationale for a "male" academy.

NOW's first claim was that Detroit was establishing schools for the purpose of single sex education that would use public funds to discriminate against females. As Sedler pointed out in his opinion, this was clearly not the case:

> The effect of the male academy is not to provide a single-sex option for male students, but to...[create] a pilot setting in which the Detroit Public Schools can evaluate the effectiveness of various curricular and other programs directed toward meeting the educational needs of inner city males (Memorandum of Opinion from Wayne State University Law School Professor Robert Sedler, to Dr. Arthur Carter, Deputy Superintendent, May 7, 1991).

We were and are of the same opinion as Attorney Robert Sedler. In fact, it is difficult to believe that anyone would thwart efforts to solve a problem of this magnitude. An analysis of the data clearly indicates that a segment of society is suffering disproportionately. Further, the Black male crisis continues to drain the resources of Detroit and the nation. We're talking billions of dollars—as many scholars and experts have indicated.

The second claim advanced by NOW was that the

curriculum of the proposed Male Academy was racist. This amounted to a gross distortion and profound lack of understanding about African-centered education. As numerous scholars and educators have pointed out, African-centered education is an effort to reach Black students by relocating the centuries-old dislocated African in America. In African-centered education, Africans and African Americans are conceptualized as subjects, not objects. The Black Experience is no longer relegated to the margins, but takes its proper place at the center of the curriculum. In this educational relocation, other cultures and experiences including that of Europeans, are included in the curriculum. Africa and African America are only the beginning; it is not the end of the educational process for Black students. Further, African-centered education has the potential to benefit all students. As Sedler said in his opinion: "What we have learned relative to the African-centered curriculum has been beneficial to all students, male/female and Black/White" (Memorandum of Opinion, 1991).

Nonetheless, NOW filed this lawsuit against the Detroit Public Schools on August 5, 1991, in the case of *Nancy Doe, et. al. v. The Detroit Board of Education of the School District of the City of Detroit*. Interestingly, but not surprisingly, NOW had difficulty finding a Detroit parent to lend her name to the lawsuit.

Although we have described a legal battle between the forces of NOW and the Detroit community, we must clarify the full situation for the historical record. NOW was joined by the American Civil Liberties Union. Further, some segments of the Civil Rights community, both privately and publicly, took a position against the Male Academy. Traditionally integrationist in their approach to Black Liberation, some Civil Rights activists argued that a Male Academy, unlike the segregated schools of the Old South, did not evolve from racist and unequal educational opportunities.

Despite the thorough and excellent defense presented by Professor and Attorney Robert Sedler and the Board's law firm—Lewis, Whit and Clay—Judge George E. Woods ruled against the Detroit School District on August 15, 1991, granting a preliminary injunction that delayed the opening of Detroit's three male academies for three weeks. On November 7, 1991, Judge Woods dismissed the action which had been brought by NOW and the ACLU against the Detroit School Board after the District and its adversaries signed a settlement agreement that "the Academies will be operated as schools which are open to both sexes in their enrollment, programs and admissions, policies and procedures..." (*Stipulation and Agreement,* No. 91-CV-73821, p.2).

Judge Woods' ruling appears to be based on a pure constructionist presentation of the law. Certainly, there have been situations where the law was subordinated to the needs of the larger society, such as in Brown vs. Board of Education. Further, a ruling by the U.S. Court of Appeals for the Fourth Circuit allowed the European American Virginia Military Institute (VMI) to continue to operate on an all-male basis. Although VMI's case has been appealed to the U.S. Supreme Court, which may or may not overturn the lower Court's ruling, the point remains that justice is not blind; she peeks when decisions involve African Americans, particularly those who are economically displaced.

The Detroit community did not accept Judge Wood's ruling. The compromise between the Board and NOW was to have the three Academies admit girls such that each would have a 30% female population. In order to comply with this order, Detroit parents would have to complete applications to enroll their girls. This did not and has not occurred to any great extent. The Detroit community had picketed and protested against NOW's lawsuit throughout the preliminary hearing that resulted in the granting of an injunction against the District. Community groups and community coalitions were formed and met on a regular basis to mount their protest campaign and to organize a city-wide effort to effectively "defeat" NOW's legal "victory." This community action resulted in the three Academies having an overwhelmingly male population in 1991 and so it remains today.

In actuality, neither the Male Academy Task Force, nor the School Board, nor, certainly, Watson and Smitherman, had ever intended to deny equal access to quality education for Detroit's girls. In fact, toward the end of the Male Academy Task Force's deliberations, the groundwork was being laid for the next phase: the creation of a Female Academy, which was to have a science and math focus. This proposal has since eventuated in the establishment of the Mae C. Jemison Academy (after the first Black woman astronaut), which is delivering a science curriculum with an African-centered educational philosophy.

After the court case, Detroit's Male Academies opened to a great deal of local and national media attention. Watson was invited to appear on various television talk shows and to speak at several seminars around the country. One such appearance, in particular, deserves elaboration: the discussion on Ted Koppel's *Nightline*. Watson, a NOW representative, and Kwame Kenyatta, presently a member of the Detroit School Board, were the discussants. What came across during this program was the collective effort of the Detroit community—parents and school personnel working together to make change in our community.

PROFILE OF MALCOLM X ACADEMY'S
STUDENTS

The Academy's student body the first year and in
subsequent years continue to reflect the will of the Detroit
Black community, namely, a school to uplift and empower
its at-risk young males. While all three academies have
some females, the population remains overwhelmingly male.

Year	# of Males	# of Females
1991-92	155	11
1992-93	388	59
1993-94	418	76

THE STRUGGLE CONTINUES

*Why would they name the school after
him? [Malcolm X] He was a racist and a hate-
monger. Even the name Coleman Young would
be better than that.*—Middle aged white male
resident of Warrendale Community in Detroit,
1992. [At that time, Coleman Young, Detroit's
first Black Mayor, had been in office for nearly
twenty years, and for most of these years, he had
been the object of resentment, and sometimes,
hatred from whites —Authors].

In the summer of 1992, a year after Malcolm X had
been established, the Detroit Board of Education decided to
move the Academy to permanent quarters. Throughout its
first year, the school had been housed on the first floor of
Woodward Elementary School, but there was a huge waiting
list for Malcolm X. Furthermore, both Malcolm X and the

51

school whose space it shared, Woodward Elementary, had large enrollments. The two schools could not occupy the same building. The Board made the decision to move the Academy to the Leslie Elementary School building, which had been vacant for some time, but which, unlike other closed school buildings in the city, was in pretty good shape and would not require extensive renovation. There was one drawback: the site chosen was in Warrendale, an older neighborhood on Detroit's lower west side that was over 75% white. The news of an all-Black African-centered Male Academy did not sit well with local white residents. As Principal of the Malcolm X Academy, it was Watson who would have to face the virulent anger and racist fury of Warrendale residents. He recalls his reaction to their reaction:

> When I was growing up in the late 1960's, I remember watching how Black people were treated in the South. I remember Civil Rights demonstrators being bitten by dogs, being hosed down with water, and being called every name in the book. But what sticks out in my mind most is how white people would sit out on their porches in extremely hot temperatures and watch with utter contempt and disgust on their faces as Black people passed through the streets. It was as though they wanted us all to go back to Africa.
>
> I attended a meeting along with several Detroit School officials at a local community church center in Warrendale. There were very few dark faces in the standing-room-only crowd. Inside, the atmosphere was Klan-like. Outside, it was like a page from the '60s down South. People were sitting on porches in their short sleeves, drinking beer.

The meeting Watson refers to had been called by the Detroit School Board and newly-hired Superintendent, Dr. Deborah McGriff, to talk with local residents about the move of Malcolm X Academy into the Warrendale area. The chairperson of the Warrendale Association seemed to be a woman of moral integrity. She was doing her best to get the unruly, racist crowd to listen to reason. They would not. They talked in small groups, ignoring the chairperson. Some said we should "send those niggers back to Africa." Most felt that the Detroit Board of Education had no right putting this Academy into "their" neighborhood. Others argued that the local community should have had some input in the decision. No mention was made of the several Detroit School Board meetings—all of which, by Michigan law, must be open to the public—during which the move of Malcolm X Academy was discussed. Of course, the truth of the matter was that, like most of Detroit's 20% white population, few of these Warrendale residents had school-age children, or if they did, those children attended private schools. Thus they rarely, if ever, attended any meetings of the Detroit Board of Education.

It was intriguing to listen to some of the speakers raving on and on about why they didn't want the Malcolm X Academy in their neighborhood. Some felt that since it was a predominately male school, the students would break into their homes. Others wanted metal detectors installed in the Academy so students could be checked for guns. Nobody paid any attention to the fact that in the Academy's first year, all the students were only kindergarten through fifth grade.

Prior to the opening of school that year, several more meetings with Warrendale residents were held; the same negative atmosphere prevailed. Eventually, their racism and resistance escalated to the point where they started damaging the school building. The District had to put officers on twenty-four hour duty in the building. Despite the heavy security, they managed to paint a swastika on the building.

On the opening day of school, it was like Little Rock revisited. Police helicopters flew above the building, SWAT teams were in place, and Detroit Police Department officers and cars were on patrol. One would have thought the President of the United States was coming to Malcolm X Academy. Although there were no major incidents, on the bus ride home, a group of white males attacked the Academy's buses with raw eggs. Malcolm X Academy parents had attempted to prepare their children for such irrational and racist behavior, but still, many of the students were frightened. After all, they were only little boys, five, six and seven years old—and they weren't carrying guns.

Chapter Five

PHILOSOPHY, CURRICULUM AND PEDAGOGY AT MALCOLM X

AFRICAN-CENTERED EDUCATION

The mission of the Malcolm X Academy grows out of its grounding in the pedagogy that has come to be known as "African Immersion," or "Afrocentricity." Simply stated, African-centered education approaches knowledge from the perspective of Africa as the origin of human civilization and the descendants of Africans as subjects, rather than objects, of history and scientific observation. While focus is on African and African American culture, the pedagogy is multicultural and includes study of all groups in the historical and cultural presence of the United States and the world. Those who know history will recognize today's African-centered educational movement as the continuance of the educational tradition established by our late elders, Drs. Carter G. Woodson (1933) and W.E.B. DuBois (1903;1933) Both of these scholars (Harvard-trained, as it turns out) advocated the necessity for Black Americans to uncover the truths about our African origins and to correct the distortions of our history, before, during, and after enslavement in the U.S. Further, DuBois and Woodson stressed that we must re-program our thinking which, as Woodson put it over half a century ago, had been corrupted by "miseducation."

What is new about today's African-centered education

is the struggle to institutionalize this approach in the early years of school. Previous educational efforts were sporadic and aimed at higher levels of schooling. For instance, even the crucial movement for Black Studies in the 1960's focused on African-centered education in colleges, universities, and, occasionally high schools. It's been a long time coming, but there is now a widespread consensus among Black parents and educators that the salvation of African American children—especially, African American males—must begin on the pre-school and early elementary school levels. Research and experience clearly indicate that, without intervention, Black students start to fall off in educational performance long before they enter high school. The drop-off period begins around fourth grade. Many Black male students never make it to high school, and all too often, those who do make it are behind in grade level and academic performance in crucial subjects, like reading and math.

> I remember being on a natural high when I finally got the chance to teach some Black students the works of Black authors, and especially my man, DuBois and his powerful *Souls of Black Folk.* This particular group of young folk had put their lives on the line in a tense show-down with college administrators because they wanted to learn about "us and the Bloods who went before," as they put it. There were a lot of Brothas in this group, too, hungry for self-knowledge and committed to re-educating themselves. But when we got down to the nitty-gritty of our work, it was painful and frustrating for all of us. The educational system had short-changed them, not only by miseducating them about us, but also by failing to provide them with the basic tools of literacy

that would have enabled them to read the words
of our elders from whom they were so eager to
learn.

Teaching that class was one of the hardest
things I've ever done. Some days I would just
go home and cry. Some days I felt like
committing murder.

—Geneva Smitherman,
Memoirs of a Daughter in the Hood

Educators committed to African-centered education are
trying to work out pragmatic ways to operationalize this
philosophy while teaching the traditional "three r's" to
students. What does it mean to teach beginning reading,
elementary arithmetic, basic science, etc., from the
perspective of Africa as the center and African/African
Americans as subjects? How can we "set afoot a new man"
who understands that education is not just about making a
living but making a life? As Dubois said back in 1933, the
function of education is not to "make men carpenters, but to
make carpenters men." Today in the 1990's, Dr. Carol Lee
is profoundly instructive on this point. A pioneering
educator, Dr. Lee co-founded one of the first independent
Black elementary schools with an African-centered focus.
She has amassed twenty-five years of experience blending
theory and practice in African-centered education. Lee says,
"Just because one is knowledgeable about Black history and
culture and likes children does not mean one can effectively
teach using an African-centered pedagogy" (1992, 167).
Lee, et.al. have outlined ten principles of an African-
Centered pedagogy:

1. The social ethics of African culture as
   exemplified in the social philosophy
   of Maat;

57

2. The history of the African continent and Diaspora;

3. The need for political and community organizing within the African American community;

4. The positive pedagogical implications of the indigenous language, African American English;

5. Child development principles that are relevant to the positive and productive growth of African American children;

6. African contributions in science, mathematics, literature, the arts and societal organization;

7. Teaching techniques that are socially interactive, holistic and positively affective;

8. The need for continuous personal study (and critical thinking);

9. The African principle that "children are the reward of life";

10. The African principle of reciprocity . . that is, a teacher sees his or her own future symbiotically linked to the development of students.

MISSION AND CURRICULUM

Malcolm X Academy was established as an African-centered program, stressing multicultural, humanistic, and futuristic education. The Academy seeks to create students who will achieve academic excellence, while developing ethnic awareness, pride, and high self-esteem. In its mission statement, the Academy articulates the following objectives and goals:

* Students will learn to read beginning in pre-school
* Students will be exposed to computer technology
* Students will learn Kiswahili, Spanish, and French
* Students will participate in vocational technology
* Students will not experience failure
* Students will be put in accelerated programs
(Malcolm X Academy, 1991, 3)

Additional features of the educational program are the following:

* African and African American literature, history, and culture
* Rites of Passage
* Peer tutoring and counseling ("Each one, teach one")
* Community and civic responsibility ("Umoja Karamu")
* Community and university male mentoring programs
* Mathematics and science, including Black contributors
* Emphasis on personal discipline, social adjustment, and self-control
* Homework at least three days per week
* Uniforms and strict dress code
* Aerospace program
* Drafting
* Saturday School
* Eleven-month school year
* Extended school day

* No special education track
* Parent pledge of a minimum three
    hours per month to Academy;
    the signing of a covenant to
    support the Malcolm X
    program.

The Academy opened with a kindergarten-through-fifth-grade population. The projection was to add a grade a year up until the eighth-grade. The Academy launched its first eighth-grade class in September, 1994. Thus, Black male students in Detroit can now get their "basic training," from kindergarten through eighth-grade, in Malcolm X's African-centered environment before passing on to high school, which begins in the ninth grade in Detroit.

The Academy's philosophy is to fit the curriculum to the child and to create a school climate that deals with the whole child—mentally, emotionally, and cognitively. If males are more aggressive, this aggression is not punished. Rather, it's accepted, and discipline is meted out with love, not punitiveness that makes the child feel something is inherently "wrong" with him. Further, as indicated above, there is a strict dress code at the Academy, in order to cut down on distractions from the educational process. This means not only uniform dress, but no designer haircuts, no tails or earrings for boys, no lit-up gym shoes, and definitely no $200 designer sneakers.

Early on, the Academy had to confront a major problem facing public school districts committed to an African-centered educational philosophy: the dearth of texts and teaching material that are age-appropriate and pedagogically grounded in Afrocentricity. The parents and staff found blatant shortcomings and omissions in the core texts typically used in public schools throughout the country. Consider, for instance, the core science text used at the fourth-grade level. This is a book that contains over 300 pages, with no graphic or pictorial representations of African American scientists. Various sections of this core text provide biographical sketches of European scientists but neglect commensurate information about African American scientists who have made similar contributions. For example, there is a profile about Dr. Gladys Anderson, a European American nutritionist who has done extensive research in food nutrition. Here would have been an opportunity to include information on Dr. Lloyd Hall, an African American scientist, who developed innovative techniques for food preservation, and the refrigeration techniques for transporting food across the country.

The fundamental strategy for correcting the blatantly biased character of the core texts is infusion, either through the use of supplemental texts (though these are still few in number), or through the incorporation of research from academic sources (which requires the development of lesson plans that "translate" such material to the elementary school level). As an example of the first type of infusion, Malcolm X's staff has successfully utilized *Afro-American Pioneers in Science* (Watson, 1984), which provides information about twelve African American scientists, and at the same time teaches scientific concepts relative to the work and contributions of these scientists. Included are such scientific pioneers as Dr. Meredith Gordine, who developed the electro gas dynamics channel which converts gas into electricity, and Dr. Ernest Just who did extensive work in cellular research. An example of infusing research data from academic sources is the Academy's use of the African American Baseline Essays (Portland Public Schools, 1987), which provide extensive essays in the major subject areas studied in school: math, science, English, and social studies.

By and large, though, because of the lack of core textbooks and curriculum material, coupled with institutionalized racism in the educational system, teachers must develop their own material if they are to impart an African-centered curriculum to public school students. Since 1991, Malcolm X Academy staff have been expending tremendous time and energy developing African-centered, age and grade-appropriate lesson plans and teaching material for their students. The following are sample lesson plans.

LANGUAGE DEVELOPMENT—SPANISH
GRADES 4-7

TEACHER: VICTOR GIBSON

I. *Objective:* Motivating African American students to appreciate and understand the historical connection between English-speaking Africans and Spanish-speaking Africans.

II. *Socialization Theory*—The society in which children are raised will be reflected in their language and their cultural attitudes.

Establish the connection between Africans who speak English (because they were socialized in colonies of England) with Africans who speak Spanish (because they were socialized in a Hispanic culture).

III. *Prior Knowledge:* Diaspora of Africans—15th-16th centuries.

IV. *Geography of:* Atlantic Ocean, Gulf of Mexico,

Cuba, Mexico, Central and South America.

V. *Politics:* African American political refugees.

VI. *Vocabulary*

Spanish Verbs: hablar   -to speak
venir   -to come
estar   -to be (temporary)
ser   -to be (permanent)
vivir   -to live

Spanish Pronouns: Yo, tú, él, ella, usted-singular, nosotros, vosotros, ellos, ellas, ustedes-plural

Spanish Greetings: ¿Hola, Qué tal? Buenos días, ¿ Como esta usted?

STUDENTS WILL BE ABLE TO:

1. Chart the movement of the African slave trade to the Caribbean, Central and South Americas.
2. Understand the African-American political refugee flight to Cuba and Mexico.
3. Conjugate Spanish verbs in the present and past tenses.

   Yo hablo-I speak   Yo hablé-I spoke
   Yo vengo-I can   Yo vine-I came
   Yo estoy-I am   Yo estuve-I was

4. Exchange basic greetings with other students in Spanish.

Hola	Hola
¿ Como te llamas?	Me llamo
¿ Como esta usted?	Yo estoy bien, gracias
Buenos dias	Buenos días
Adios	Adios

Activities: Students will read and study a map of the world. Examples: students will read about the influence of African culture in Cuba today; they will learn about the Black Panther Party and political refugees in Cuba; they will explore similarities between heroes of African and Hispanic heritage. Students will speak in Spanish to other students. Students will label home objects using Spanish vocabulary.

BUILDING SELF ESTEEM

TEACHER: COZETTE SPINNER

I. *Objective:* Increased self-esteem and positive interaction between students.

STUDENTS WILL BE ABLE TO:
Speak and perform positive actions towards classmates.
Receive positive actions from classmates.
Begin thinking more positively while at school.

II. *Materials:*

a. sparkle forms: (The sparkle form is a star shaped like a sparkle. The star form has a picture of a famous African American, such as Malcolm X, Martin Luther King Jr., etc. The stars are placed in the students' bags; they collect the stars, and the teacher rewards them with play money which can be spent at the school's store.)
b. brown bags
c. play dollars (made by teacher)
d. items purchased from dollar store
e. sheet with positive saying, one per child
f. each student has a hanger at his desk; he places photos of himself at different stages in his life on the hanger, for example, beginning with his baby picture.

III. *Activities:*

Teacher explains procedure. All students will decorate brown bag and tape to desk. Stars will be given, five to each student per week for four weeks. Write a saying on it which you would want someone to say to you, and place in another person's bag sometime during the day. Try to choose a bag of a student who is not your good friend, especially one who you don't know well. Same with play dollars, three per week. Use sheet provided by teacher to select positive phrase. Watch for smile on person's face. Say something nice and out-of-the-ordinary during the rest of the day in other classes.

Bring pictures of yourself to share the with rest of class, so that we can and will know more about you. The more we can see that is positive, the more positive we'll become. Make picture mobile, hang in room for classmates to see.

Teacher observation and "ME" mobiles.

MATH
TEACHER: MARVIN BODLEY

Lesson #1

I. *Objective:* Students will be able to demonstrate how the Egyptians found their orientation (direction).

II. *Materials:* Textbook, "The African Roots of Mathematics," by Deborah Moore, pp. 63-67, compass, map of Africa, ruler, calculator, pencil and paper, overhead projector, transparencies.

III. *Method:* Students will read and discuss pages 63-67 of text. Students will use compass and map to demonstrate direction calculation.

IV. *Evaluation:* Students will demonstrate an 80% efficiency in demonstrating how Egyptians calculated directions.

Lesson #2

I. *Objective:* Students will be able to calculate a ship's wavelength when giving information depicting wave speed and period calculations.

II. *Materials:* Textbook pp. 71-72; calculator, paper and pencil.

III. *Method: Word Problems:* Queen Hatsheput's expedition to the land of Punt may have encountered waves with a period of 10 seconds and a wave speed of 15.6 meters per second (mps). What is the wavelength?

Answer: period = p = 10
                                     wave speed = w = 15.6
                                     wave length = v

                         wave speed = wavelength/period

$$w = \frac{v}{p}$$

$15.6 = \frac{v}{10}$ cross multiply

15.6 x 10 = v
156 = v meters/second
(156 wave lengths per second (wps)

IV. *Evaluation:* Students must demonstrate an 80%
efficiency in calculation of various data.

LEWIS HOWARD LATIMER

TEACHER: CLIFFORD WATSON

I. *Objective:* Students will be able to understand what Lewis Latimer did to develop the patent drawing for the light bulb filament.

II. *Materials:* Teacher resource materials: Hunter Adams III, "African and African American Contributions to Science and Technology," Portland Baseline Essays (Portland Public Schools, 1987).

III. *Vocabulary:*

1. Inventor
2. Filament
3. Carbon
4. Inexpensive
5. Draftsman
6. Patent
7. Economical
8. Incandescent

IV. *Design:*

Students should be introduced to the vocabulary words.

Students should define each vocabulary word.

Students should use the dictionary and the text to look up the definitions of words.

Students should put each word into a logical sentence.

All students should have an opportunity to read

their sentences to the class.

V. *Procedures:*
  1. Tell the students that we are going to learn about
     Lewis Latimer, an African American who
     developed a process to improve the light
     bulb.
  2. Explain to the students that the carbon filament
     made the light bulb last longer, making it
     more economical.
  3. Develop information sheets on Latimer. Have
     the students take turns reading the
     information from the resource sheets.

VI. *Discussion Question:* What were two of Lewis
     Latimer's inventions? (Carbon filament and
     incandescent light).

VII. *Out-of-Class Assignment:* Have students write an
      essay about the life of Lewis Latimer.

AFROCENTRIC PROGRAMS AND
CELEBRATIONS

It is necessary to provide African-centered alternatives to the many Eurocentric holidays rooted in historical distortions and over-emphasized consumption—e.g., Thanksgiving and Christmas. Changing the school culture now requires rituals to balance the distortions Black youth are exposed to outside of school.

In reference to America's Thanksgiving Day, Barashango (1979) notes that this is a "celebration of horror" which commenced in the so-called "New World" with the near-total extermination of an entire race of people (the "Indians") and the enslavement of Africans (1979, 1). Although the "Amer-Indians were very friendly and hospitable" to the Pilgrims and taught them how to fish and plant corn, these "intruding European settlers" repaid the Indians by stealing from them, subjecting them to cruel mistreatment, and eventually resorting to massacre (1979, 3-16). Rather than continue this miseducation, Malcolm X Academy instituted "Umoja Karamu," a unity feast of Thanksgiving, celebrating Black family and community unity. The celebration was conceived by Mr. Edward Simms, Jr., of Philadelphia and observed at Richard Allen City in Philadelphia in 1971, and at Banneker Village in Washington, D.C. later the same year (Barashango, 1979, 52). Students at the Academy celebrated their first annual Umoja Karamu by raising money to purchase food and blankets for Detroit's homeless. They donated over 300 blankets and 1500 canned goods to Detroit's Perpetual Mission, founded and managed by Mother Charleszetta Waddells, and to Detroit's Operation Get-Down, under the leadership of Mr. Bernard Parker.

As another Afrocentric ritual, instead of Halloween, Malcolm X students highlight and celebrate traditional African/African American heroes in an "All-Saints Day" recognition. Finally, instead of what Barashango calls the "merry mess" of Christmas (1979, 58), the Academy celebrates Kwanzaa, an ancient African celebration, common to many societies on the African Continent. Kwanzaa focuses on working together and the harvesting of "first fruits," and was resurrected and established from an African American perspective by Dr. Maulana (Ron) Karenga in 1966. The Academy emphasizes that Kwanzaa is not a "Black Christmas"; rather, it is intended to celebrate the African American cultural heritage, Black family, and community unity.

COMPREHENSIVE ATHLETIC PROGRAM

If you survey most urban Black males and ask them what they want to be when they "grow up," they'll tell you a basketball player. At the Malcolm X Academy, this pattern of thinking is not dismissed; rather we capitalize on it. The Academy is the only Detroit elementary school to participate in a competitive, comprehensive athletic program—basketball, baseball and track teams. Students can participate only if they meet two requirements:

      1) They must have a 2.5 grade point
         average;
      2) They must have a (1) or (2) in
         citizenship.

The Academy seeks to produce student-athletes, with emphasis on students. For example, during 1992-93, one student who was a star player on the baseball team got into a fight. The team made the play-offs, but this student was dropped from the team until his citizenship improved. He subsequently went from the lowest—a (3)-in citizenship to the highest—a (1), and he received awards and commendations from several teachers.

STAFF

The Academy's staff includes both male and female teachers and administrators. While there is an emphasis on male role models, this gender mix has proved very effective and valuable in the experience of students since the Academy's inception in 1991. The chart below provides a profile of the teaching staff over the past three years.

	#Male	#Fem	#Black	#White
1991-92	7	3	8	2
1992-93	12	14	23	3
1993-94	14	12	22	4
1994-95	11	16	24	3

As Malcolm X grows and evolves, the teaching staff continues to be comprised of young and older teachers, both in terms of age and experience. All have a Bachelor's degree, about one-third have Master's degrees, and a few are working toward the Ph.D. It has tended to be the case that the male teachers have either come from other professions or graduated with college degrees in fields other than education. For example, the current math teacher, who produced an outstanding group of seventh grade math performers, left General Motors for teaching. The teaching staff is not entirely certified, and several teachers are working toward certification. All have demonstrated a serious commitment to African-centered education and are unequivocally dedicated to the education of Black males.

In terms of administrators, there has consistently been a female assistant principal and a male principal, Clifford Watson. Currently, the assistant principal has 23 years of teaching experience, and the principal has 14 years as a teacher and 9 years as a principal. In 1993-94, there were both a female and a male counselor. Other staff in that school year included a male educational technician/coordinator, a female secretary, and a male and a female maintenance worker.

"MY BROTHER'S KEEPER": MALCOLM X ACADEMY AND MICHIGAN STATE UNIVERSITY (MSU) IN PARTNERSHIP

"My Brother's Keeper" is a mentoring program for male elementary-school students in the Detroit Public Schools which uses MSU Black students as mentors. The Program was conceptualized by Smitherman in consultation with and based on concepts developed by Watson. The goals of "My Brother's Keeper" are to convey to students at a young age the empowerment to be gained through a college education, and to promote educational self-esteem and community responsibility. The Program was first launched in 1990 at Woodward Elementary School, where Watson was principal. In addition to Woodward, the Program operated at Loving Elementary School. In 1991, it was introduced at the Malcolm X Academy and has operated solely at the Academy since that time.

Black students at MSU, many of them products of the 'hoods of the nation, are matched with the Academy students. The MSU mentors take field trips and work with their mentees on Saturdays at their school. Some days the students visit with their mentors at MSU where they may tour the campus, attend a class or two with their mentors, eat lunch in the residence hall cafeterias, and generally "hang out" with their mentors to get an introduction to college life. As a bonus for achievement, for the past two summers, a selected group of Malcolm X students have spent a week in residence at Michigan State University. Future plans are to institutionalize this feature of the Program and to expand the group.

Each "Brother's Keeper" session begins with a recitation by mentors and mentees of "My Brother's Keeper" pledge. It encompasses all of the goals of the Program: to encourage students not only to work hard in school, but also to become socially responsible by caring about themselves and each other:

> **We will work hard**
> **We will gain knowledge**
> **We will share**
> **We will be kind to each other**
> **We will love and take care of each**
> **other**
> **We will learn to become our own**
> **brother's and sister's keeper**

"RITES OF PASSAGE"

The Academy's "Rites of Passage" Program is conducted by Kabaz (Black Jewels), an independent community organization in Detroit. "Rites of Passage" is a cultural ritual developed to guide young people through passages or stages of their lives, to ensure a successful transition and entry into a new life situation. For African

American males, "Rites of Passage" is a life jacket to those who are historically and culturally drowning. Participants learn to see themselves as a seed in the universe and as part of the cosmic whole.

The Program is a nine-month "passage" for boys and girls in the seventh grade. They are required to participate for two hours during the school day and for three hours on Saturday mornings. The "Year of Passage" has the following components: Afrocentric didactics—e.g., manhood responsibilities, self identity and personality formation; drill team, for disciplined training with a cultural motif; woodshop; tie-dye; family tree research; and field trips. These activities culminate in a "Rites of Passage" ceremony attended by family members, teachers, and the community-at-large to honor the students and recognize their passage from one status to another. Students must learn the principles of Nguzo Saba and write a paper demonstrating how they can manifest these concepts in the community. They are taught community responsibility by involvement in outreach projects, such as working with senior citizens; some participants tutor first-and-second-graders at the Academy and at the Nation of Islam mosque (which has adopted the Academy).

LOCAL SCHOOL COMMUNITY
ORGANIZATION (LSCO)

Parental participation and involvement is a sine qua non of African-centered Education ("It takes a whole village to raise a child"). The parents' group at Malcolm X Academy is particularly supportive of the African-centered program at the school. Although attendance at some school-related events is somewhat low, as is typical for urban schools, parents have, on occasion, filled up the Academy's auditorium. Further, some parents have exceeded the covenant of three (3) hours per month devoted to activities at the school. Parents serve as hall monitors and tutors. Some attend field trips and school outings as chaperones; for instance, on the Academy's trips to Toronto and New York. Several parents have driven their own and other children to school events, without any compensation for mileage; other parents have devoted time and energy to caring for the Academy's choir robes and students' uniforms.

LSCO activities include monthly seminars, with guest speakers, to train and empower parents in the meaning and significance of African-centered education. Speakers have included Dr. Betty Shabazz, Dr. Leonard Jeffries, and Minister Louis Farrakhan.

Chapter Six

AMANDALA!: STUDENT ACHIEVEMENT AT MALCOLM X

Detroit may not be providing all of the students with equal opportunities, or access to opportunities," the [Detroit Public Schools' Office of Research, Evaluation and Testing] report said. "Evidence which is available indicates that schools of choice cannot be seen as a panacea for improving student achievement.

On the other hand, student attendance, grades, parental involvement and teacher satisfaction were cited as strengths in the study...Several schools, such as the African-Centered Malcolm X Academy, bucked the achievement trend, registering test-score gains in reading and math (Russell, 1994).

Overcoming the odds, and in the face of the many obstacles it has had to confront over the past three years, Detroit's Malcolm X Academy is well on its way to being a successful educational program for empowering young Black males.

As mentioned, when the Task Force set its implementation guidelines for the Male Academy, it articulated the goals set forth in the District's Quality Education Plan. The "proof of the pudding" for the Malcolm X Academy was to be the following:

1) performance in reading and math scores as

measured by the nationally standardized California Achievement Test (CAT);

    2) adherence to the student disciplinary code, as measured by the yearly percent of student code violations, and;

    3) attendance.

    At the end of its first year of operation, the Academy was well on its way to achieving the Superintendent's designation as an "excellent" school.

CALIFORNIA ACHIEVEMENT TEST (CAT) SCORES IN READING AND MATH

    The District's goal in terms of reading and math, "core" subjects, is for 75% of the students to perform at or above grade level on the California Achievement Test. The table below presents the year-end CAT results for students from the first year of the Academy's operation, 1991-92.

CAT SCORES
(June 1992)

GRADE	SUBJECT	SCORE
Kindergarten	Reading	MDNP 63%*
(n=28)	Math	MDNP 62%
First	Reading	2.0**
(n=23)	Math	2.1
Second	Reading	3.2
(n=29)	Math	2.8

GRADE	SUBJECT	SCORE
Third	Reading	5.0
(n=28)	Math	8.1
Fourth	Reading	3.9
(n=31)	Math	5.0
Fifth	Reading	5.4
(n=27)	Math	6.5

The first year's pattern of performance continued into the Academy's second year. It is interesting to note CAT scores of the boys enrolled in the Academy's two all-male fifth grade classes in 1992-93. In particular, note the number of boys scoring above fifth grade level in both reading and math.

---

*MDNP is the Median Normative Percentile score on these nationally standardized tests of math and reading. The score reflects the students' performace in comparision to other kindergartners across the nation. In this instance, the score indicates that only 37% of the kindergartners across the country scored higher in reading than the Malcolm students.

**This score ranks the students' performance in terms of grade level and, where applicable, months beyond grade level. Thus, the reading score of "2.0" means that the Malcolm X first graders were reading at the second grade level; the math score of "2.1" means that the Malcolm X first graders' math performance was one month beyond the second grade level.

GRADE FIVE, SECTION THREE
(N=27)

	CAT Reading	CAT Math
Mean Score	6.81	6.53
# Scoring at 5th gr. lvl.	6	7
# Scoring below 5th gr. lvl.	3	6
# Scoring at 6th gr. lvl.	6	3
# Scoring at 7th gr. lvl.	6	5
# Scoring at 8th gr. lvl.	4	3
# Scoring at 9th gr. lvl.	1	3
# Scoring at 10th gr. lvl.	1	0
Total in class	27	27

In terms of citizenship for this group, only one student received a failing grade of 3. All others received either 1's or 2's.

GRADE FIVE, SECTION FOUR
(N=27)

	CAT READING	CAT MATH
Mean Score	5.26	5.75
# Scoring at 5th gr. level	8	7
# Scoring below 5th	10	7
# Scoring at 6th gr. level	7	9
# Scoring at 7th gr. level	1	4
# Scoring at 8th gr. level	1	0

In terms of citizenship for this class, only two students received a failing grade of 3. All others received 1's or 2's in citizenship.

It was not only the fifth grade all-male classes that have been outstanding; at every grade level, and in both reading and math, the majority of Malcolm X students have scored at or above the national norm on the California Achievement Test. The table below presents the CAT math scores in 1992-93 for Malcolm X and for the Detroit School District as a whole:

1992-93 CALIFORNIA ACHIEVEMENT TEST— MATH: PERCENT OF STUDENTS AT OR ABOVE NATIONAL NORM-BY GRADE LEVEL

Grade level	1st	2nd	3rd	4th	5th	6th
Malcolm X Schl Dist.	84	94	84	78	70	86
Average	71	58	54	48	46	37

(Source: Moore & Associates, 1994, 18)

A comparison of the Academy and the District in reading is also revelatory. Again, the Academy is higher overall. The table below presents the California Achievement Test Grade Equivalency Scores in reading for Malcolm X and the District for 1992-93:

1992-93 CALIFORNIA ACHIEVEMENT TEST—READING: EQUIVALENCY SCORES

Grade level	1st	2nd	3rd	4th	5th	6th
Malcolm X	1.7	3.7	4.1	5.9	5.6	7.5
District Avg.	1.8	2.7	3.7	4.2	5.6	6.1

(Source: Moore & Associates, 1994, 25)

Finally, it is interesting to compare achievement at Malcolm X with that of another Detroit school, a "comparison group," with a similar poverty index and other comparable demographics. According to a report from the outside consulting firm hired to evaluate Detroit's three male academies, "with the exception of fifth-grade reading and math CAT-GE scores, Malcolm X students' performance was consistently superior to comparison group students in CAT scores, GPAs, and attendance" (Moore & Associates, 1994, 44). The following tables present California Achievement Test results for Malcolm X Academy and the comparison group.

CALIFORNIA ACHIEVEMENT TEST— READING: PERCENT OF STUDENTS AT OR ABOVE NATIONAL NORM BY GRADE

	% By Grade Level		
	3rd	4th	5th
Malcolm X	59	81	51
Comparison Group	46	38	46

CALIFORNIA ACHIEVEMENT TEST— MATH: PERCENT OF STUDENTS AT OR ABOVE NATIONAL NORM BY GRADE

	% By Grade Level		
	3rd	4th	5th
Malcolm X	84	78	70
Comparison Group	46	52	62

CALIFORNIA ACHIEVEMENT TEST— READING: MEAN EQUIVALENCY SCORES BY GRADE

	Mean Grade Equivalency		
	3rd	4th	5th
Malcolm X	4.1	5.9	5.6
Comparison Group	3.6	4.2	5.8

CALIFORNIA ACHIEVEMENT TEST MATH: MEAN GRADE EQUIVALENCY SCORES BY GRADE

	Mean Grade Equivalency		
	3rd	4th	5th
Malcolm X	5.3	5.8	7.2
Comparison Group	3.6	4.4	7.4

In the third year of the Academy's operation, 1993-94, there was an outstanding achievement in math performance by the seventh-grade class (N=61). (Malcolm X is the only of the three Male Academies that has seventh-grade.) This achievement was evidenced on the MEAP exam, a state-wide test. Michigan is one of several states with a mandate that each school district must administer, on an annual basis, a battery of standardized tests developed by the State Board of Education. Known as the Michigan Assessment of Educational Progress (MEAP), the tests measure student achievement in several school subjects. In 1993-94, in the math MEAP, Malcolm X Academy's seventh-graders outscored all other seventh-graders in the Detroit Public School District. Of the 61 students taking the test, none scored on the lowest of the three levels of performance groupings used by the MEAP, and 93.4% scored in the top grouping. On the state-wide level, this achievement demonstrates that Malcolm X's seventh-graders outperformed their peers in such economically privileged suburban districts as Grosse Pointe, Bloomfield Hills, and Birmingham, as well as in traditional upscale academic enclaves such as Ann Arbor and East Lansing. According to an analysis of MEAP scores at empowered schools, schools of choice, and other schools throughout the state, conducted by the Detroit Free Press, "...Malcolm X Academy, an empowered school of choice received among the highest seventh-grade math scores in Michigan—second only to a gifted and talented school in Grand Rapids" (Adams, 1994).

It is important to stress that the academic results we are presenting here have been achieved at an urban public school that is predominantly Black and male. (Of the three Male Academies, Malcolm X has a slightly higher percentage of males.) The percentage of males over the three years of Malcolm X's existence is:

1991-92	1992-93	1993-94
93%	87%	85%

Further, it is important to stress that the results reported here have been achieved at a school where 67% of the student body, based on their family/household income, qualify for the federally-funded free lunch program.

DISCIPLINE

The Detroit Public School System has a code of behavioral violations and infractions warranting exclusion from school. It is the "Student Code of Conduct." The number of violations of the Code is typically high for male students in the District. The Quality Education Plan calls for student code violations of 5% or less for schools to be designated "excellent." In June of 1992, the total percent of student code violations at Malcolm X was 3%. (By contrast, the percent of violations at Woodward Elementary School, housed in the same building as Malcolm X, and with the same principal, Clifford Watson, was 17%.) This pattern of less than 5% code violations has continued.

ATTENDANCE

In many Detroit schools, attendance patterns are problematic, even on the elementary school level. The Academy's attendance in 1991-92 was good overall, and in its only all-male class that year, a fifth-grade group, the attendance was outstanding, averaging 95% for the year. The table on page 91 presents the attendance average for each student in this class.

In one of the 1992-93 all-male fifth-grade classes, this pattern of very low absenteeism also prevailed. Most of the students were absent only one or two days for the school year, and only (5) students had absences in excess of four days. In the other 1992-93 fifth grade class, absences were significantly higher by comparison although this group still managed to score above grade level on the math and reading CAT's. (This group is presently under special study to try to determine reasons for their lagging performance.)

At every grade level, Malcolm X students' daily attendance rates exceeded those of the comparison group (Moore & Associates, 50) as well as the attendance rates of the Detroit School District.

1992-93 STUDENT DAILY ATTENDANCE RATE: PERCENT OF ATTENDANCE BY GRADE

	K	1	2	3	4	5	6
Malcolm X Academy	100	97	99	100	99	100	100
District	—	92	92	94	94	94	89
Comparison Group	—	—	—	94	93	96	—

(Source: Moore & Associates, 1994, 35, 50).

ATTENDANCE, FIFTH GRADE ALL-MALE CLASS: 1991-92 STUDENT (BY I.D. NO.) AVG.% OF ATTENDANCE FOR THE YEAR

063	93%
064	91%
065	99%
066	95%
067	89%
068	96%
069	94%
070	96%
071	96%
072	97%
073	99%
074	96%
075	98%
076	96%
200	84%
201	97%
202	96%

203	96%
204	95%
205	99%
206	93%
207	84%
208	98%
209	84%
210	96%
211	100%
212	97%

EXCEPTIONAL CASES

Quantative measures, of course, cannot reveal the whole story when it comes to student performance. There continues to be exceptional cases of student achievement that the statistics and test scores don't capture. By June, 1992, the Academy could boast a number of accomplishments:

> * In the kindergarten class, one child who could not read at all in September, 1991 was reading on first grade level by June, 1992.

> * 15 of the 28 kindergarten students were reading on first grade level by June, 1992 (although Black boys are not expected to read at kindergarten level).

> * One kindergarten student had a third-grade reading comprehension level and an eighth-grade word recognition level (i.e., ability to use word attack skills) by June, 1992.

*Several kindergarten students went from "scribbling" to full-blown writing samples by the end of the 1991-92 school year.

*All except 2 of the kindergarten students had made the emotional adjustment necessary for school achievement by June, 1992.

*Several fifth-grade students had spent previous school years in emotionally-impaired classes; yet all functioned in the normal class environment at Malcolm X Academy.

*At least one student was a suicidally-prone boy who adjusted well at Malcolm X Academy.

*Several first- and second-grade students could not read pre-primers in September, 1991; all significantly improved their reading levels by June, 1992.

*In September, 1991, the fourth-grade class evidenced a diverse range of reading abilities, spanning reading levels from grades two through eight; 5-7 different reading groups were in existence throughout the school year to address this variation in reading ability; all fourth-grade students improved their reading level by June, 1992.

*In September, 1991, the fifth-grade class had 6 students reading at third-grade level and 4 at second-grade level; by June, 1992, all had improved their reading level.

*Despite a disproportionately high number of at-risk students at Malcolm X Academy the first year, as well as several "special needs"/ "special education" students [as labeled at their previous schools], and students with behavioral problems, the Academy ended the year with 75% of its students testing at or above grade level and with an average of only 3% code violations.

Other success stories can be gleaned from teachers' anecdotes about exceptional students:

When he entered Malcolm X Academy in September of 1991, Kwesi Armstrong was a fourth-grade student performing below grade level. He had low self-esteem, he had no knowledge of African American culture and he exhibited serious behavioral problems. Now a sixth grader at the Academy, Kwesi is a tutor for first-graders and an honor student. He attends after-school programs and is excelling not only in the traditional "three r's," but in African-centered Studies as well. He now has a positive attitude toward school and is a goal-setter with a clear pathway to the future.

Clarence Washburn is still not as serious as he could be, but he is a long way from where he was when he entered Malcolm X Academy in the fourth grade. He is certainly trying, and for that, we say "Sawwa, sawwa" ("right on" in

Kiswahili). At first, Clarence didn't seem interested in much of anything school-wise, and his grades reflected this disinterest. After two terms at the Academy, he has become a "B" student, and is developing greater confidence in his educational abilities. Soft-spoken and serious, there's now something in Clarence's eyes that shows his determination.

Tommy Washington came to Malcolm X Academy in third-grade, a loner and an immature cry-baby. He was very sensitive and quick to flare up in angry outbursts. By the middle of his first year at the Academy, he had been involved in fights every single week. It was our weekend trip to Toronto, Canada that marked a turning point for him. (This trip is only one of the many activities the Academy immerses our students in to broaden their horizons.) It was going to be the last chance we would take on him and the possibility that he would begin to turn around in his attitude and actions. It worked because Tommy still lights up when you just mention the Toronto trip. Now a year-and-a-half later, Tommy is becoming the young man he can be. He has a couple of friends now, he's motivated to work, the mood swings are gone, and he talks to people instead of confronting them with negative, hard feelings as he used to do. Now he even loves to hug his teacher!

Chapter Seven

It Takes a Nation of Millions to Hold Us Back

J. Edgar Hoover, and he could a' proved to ya'
He had King and X set up
Also the party with Newton, Cleaver and Seale
He ended—so get up
Time to get 'em back—You got it
Get back on the track—You got it...
Cream of the earth
And was here first
And some devils prevent this from being known
But you check out the books they own...
It's proven and fact
And it takes a nation of millions to hold us back
> —Rap Group, Public Enemy,
> "Party for Your Right to Fight,"
> from their album, *It Takes a
> Nation of Millions to Hold Us
> Back*

As the data on the educational achievement and the personal development of Malcolm X students demonstrates, Detroit's Male Academy experiment has established a track record. The proof is in the pudding. The Malcolm X program works! From a general standpoint, this success must be attributed to the collective struggle, support, and work of Malcolm X teachers, secretaries, maintenance and security personnel, technical support staff, parents, the Local School Community Organization, students, and the larger Detroit community. No lone individual can do it by him or herself. It required a team effort to implement such a program.

On a more specific level, there are several operative factors in the educational environment that account for the success of the Malcolm X Academy.

First, and fundamentally, is Malcolm X Academy's African-centered educational philosophy. We assert, without equivocation, that an African-centered educational philosophy and program can influence the attitudes, behavior, and educational performance of Black male students. This pedagogy is grounded in the human need for identity, purpose, and knowledge of self. It is an educational philosophy that is tantamount to a world view, one that speaks to the needs of the total child as a member of the human family. African-centered education links the school and the educational process to the community and the real world. The basis of learning and mastery is not simply knowledge for knowledge's sake, but knowledge for the purpose of self-empowerment and community development. Thus, an African-centered educational philosophy can ultimately be beneficial to *all* students. Given the effectiveness of our program at Malcolm X Academy, we would hope that other school districts will have the political courage and educational boldness to implement African-centered curricula and programs.

Another significant factor is the presence of male role models in the educational environment. Particularly in their formative years, African American males need and respond to male role models and authority figures. This need is especially critical for elementary-school-age boys from homes where there is no sustained male presence. At the

Malcolm X Academy, nearly 90% of the students are from single-parent, female-headed households. Obviously, there is a need and role for women in the education and development of young Black males; our point is that women cannot do it alone. To address this void and to present a unified image of Black males and females teaching together in the kindergarten-through-eighth-grade world of our students, the Malcolm X Academy made a concerted effort to bring Black males on board as teachers. In some instances, this required temporary teacher certification of Black male college graduates. In other instances, males were recruited as tutors and teacher aides.

On the very educational level where Black males have the greatest need for male teachers, there is the greatest shortage of such teachers. In fact, less than 1.5% of the nation's elementary school teachers are males of *any* color. The serious lack of Black male teachers on the elementary school level has to be addressed. One possibility would be for local governments and/or the federal government to provide scholarship incentives for males who would choose to major in elementary education. In return, they would be required to teach for a period of time, say, five years, in an urban area.

Yet, a third factor in the educational effectiveness of Malcolm X's program is our acceptance of the fact that boys and girls learn and develop differently. This has nothing to do with the myth of the inequality of the sexes; nor does it have to do with the biological differences between males and females. Rather, it is based on recognition of the differential processes involved in the early socialization of boys and girls. They develop different social habits and differing responses to environmental stimuli, because their upbringing and general socialization are different,Such differences, in turn, impact on learning styles and strategies for processing facts and information. Equality and difference can and do co-exist; being equal does not mean being the same. Recognition of such differences in no way implies deficiency. In fact, such misdirected thinking is a serious shortcoming in the European American consciousness in this country, a point made decades ago by Dr. Martin Luther King, Jr., when he said that the issue is not about the differences between Blacks and whites, but the *difference* we make of the differences.

The cultural context of Black male socialization and Black males' differential learning styles have required that we establish a receptive classroom climate at Malcolm X. Traditionally, if there's a classroom of African American males, it's been created because the students have been labeled "discipline problems" due to their "aggressiveness" and "hyperactivity." In the 1970's and 80's, these characteristics became a ticket, or automatic passage, to special education, especially in the case of Black male students. Today, the code word is "attention-deficit disorder," a 1990's rationale for creating an educational cesspool in which to dump Black boys. At the Malcolm X Academy, though, we have taken the position that the teacher needs to adjust to the child, rather than the child adjusting to the teacher. If the child can't learn the way the teacher teaches, then teach the way the child *can* learn. This has meant establishing an educational atmosphere where "aggressiveness" and "hyperactivity" are accepted as normal. Once we do that, we can move on to teach self-discipline, control, and the "three r's."

This period marks a critical juncture in the experience of Africans in America. As we approach the dawning of a new century, we find ourselves facing crisis conditions for African American males. School boards and educators must pull their heads out of the educational sand and seek creative alternatives and programs to address this crisis situation. We cannot afford to dismiss out-of-hand any *new* proposal, however "controversial" it might appear. Rather, let us examine new ideas with wisdom and objectivity.

We are fully cognizant that not every public school district permits the option of a full-scale African-Centered educational program. However, even if there is no district support of African-Centered pedagogy, there are several strategies that individual teachers can employ to capitalize on the learning potential of African-Centeredness for our students. In that spirit, we offer the following recommendations, based on our personal experiences and the recommendations of teachers at Malcolm X.

TEN-POINT CHECKLIST FOR AN
AFRICAN-CENTERED ROOM

At the very least, a teacher can create an African-Centered learning atmosphere by adorning classrooms with pictures, images, and symbols reflective of Afrocentricity. The Malcolm X Academy developed the following ten-point check-list for an African-Centered room:

1. Red, black and green flag
2. Picture(s) of the African continent
3. Picture(s) of African leaders
4. Picture(s) of Black scientists
5. Picture(s) of kings and queens of ancient Africa
6. Picture(s) of historical Black leaders
7. Picture(s) of contemporary Black leaders
8. Afrocentric current events bulletin board
9. Poster of the Malcolm X Pledge
10. Afrocentric reading center

TEACHING READING IN KINDERGARTEN

Traditionally, kindergarten for Black boys has been play, tumble and sleep. Conventional "wisdom" has been that Blacks boys don't, or won't, or can't, read at the kindergarten level. The teaching of reading in kindergarten should begin as soon as the start of school in the fall. No boys should leave kindergarten until they can read a pre-primer. Further, all students should leave kindergarten knowing the shape of the African continent. To facilitate this knowledge, a teacher can use word association, for example, a map of Africa on the students' lockers, with the word "Africa" on the map, or students' name tags in the shape of Africa. Or a picture of kente cloth, with the word "kente" on it. Or have students bring in a picture of their fathers (or any male in their family), and mount these in the classroom with the Swahili word "Baba" ("father") as a caption. Because of the lack of African-Centered reading material at this level, teachers should write their own African-Centered stories and read them to the students. Reading should be promoted as a highly valued goal to strive for, an accomplishment which students can demonstrate with pride. A photo of a Black boy, with the caption "I can read" says a lot. Numerous ideas will begin to flow about creative ways of promoting an African-Centered consciousness and reading skills once a teacher locks into this frame of mind.

PARENT INVOLVEMENT

Parents need to be informed about African-Centered education, whether or not a given school district has African-Centered curricula or not. One way would be to conduct African-Centered workshops at parent-teacher meetings. These workshops could focus on such topics as the geography of Africa or a Black historical figure. Videos dealing with the Black experience, such as *Eyes on the Prize*, could be shown and discussed. Outside speakers and resource persons could be brought in to present topics dealing with Black community life, health issues, etc. In short, there is a need to educate the parent even as we educate the son or daughter. Such education has to be on going. We are well past the day when a single month of Black history, once a year, will suffice to prepare Africans in America for life in the twenty-first century.

SCHOOL-WIDE READING PROGRAM

If there are school-district constraints on curriculum, the concept of African-Centeredness can be conveyed via an extracurricular reading program. Get readers by African American authors and expose students to books such as *African American Heroes* by Brenda Boyd (Bess Personalized Books, Inc). "Discover" your local Black bookstore. If one does not exist in your community, consult catalogues of Black bookstores and publishers and order books for the students at your school (such as Third World Press, P.O. Box 19730, Chicago, IL 60619).

ELEMENTARY SCHOOL SPORTS PROGRAM

For African American males, particularly, sports is an integral part of their environment. Many educators and lay persons devalue athletics. Some of this criticism does have merit. For example, too many Black athletes go to college and do not graduate or enter the pros. However, there are many potential Paul Robeson's (All-American football player, renown scholar, classical singer, actor) among our students. Let us expose Black males to the concept of the scholar-athlete, and rather than criticize their focus on athletics, let us capitalize on it. Integrate athletic success with academic success. Establish either a competitive sports program or an intramural one (for example, the fourth-grade vs. the fifth-grade) and require a certain level of educational achievement and citizenship for a student to participate. As mentioned, at Malcolm X Academy, we had the only elementary school competitive sports program in the Detroit Public Schools in 1993-94. Only boys who had a 2.5 grade point average or above and 1's and 2's in citizenship (i.e., satisfactory or excellent) were allowed to play on one of the sports teams.

MENTORING

Young Black boys need to be exposed to positive role models early on. The community cannot wait until its sons get to high school to begin mentoring them; many of them will have dropped out of school before they reach that level. African American community organizations can be called up to provide mentors in your school—Black Greek organizations, such as Alpha Phi Alpha and Kappa Alpha Psi exist in virtually every city; there is the Urban League, the NAACP, and a variety of community-based organizations that would be only too willing to assist if called upon. Mentors can also be older students in the same school. At Malcolm X one reason our kindergarten and first-grade students read well is that many of them have older male mentors in the upper grades at the Academy.

Finally, seek college students in nearby universities as mentors. Many Black students at these colleges are eager to give back to the communities that nurtured them. It was this impetus that led to the establishment of "My Brother's

Keeper" program at Michigan State University. In this program, Michigan State Black students make regular trips to mentor Malcolm X Academy students, thus connecting these young Black boys to older Black males successfully working toward bachelor's, master's and Ph.D. degrees. Whenever possible, the elementary school students should visit the college campus of their mentors, to get a feel for college life, so it's not something distant, foreign, or unobtainable, but a realizable possibility—they too can do like their people before them.

PARTNERSHIPS

In every community, there is a church, a community organization, a local mosque of the Nation of Islam, and a committed individual or two, all of whom are willing to help. Make contact with these community resources; they are willing to donate time, supplies, and funds because they realize that the education of our youth is everybody's business. "It takes a whole village to raise a child." At Malcolm X Academy, we have formed a partnership with Muhammad's Mosque #1. With their help, and that of local businessmen "partners," the Academy has established a college scholarship fund, to provide $10,000 in scholarships to students who meet the Malcolm X criteria (a grade point average of 3.0 or higher, 1's in citizenship, no Student Code of Conduct violations). Our first winner was Malcolm X fifth-grader, Samuel Russell.

"It's been a long time coming, but our change done come," as that classical Black song puts it. The Malcolm X Academy program, three years into its existence as a kindergarten-through-eighth-grade empowered Detroit Public School, has shown that with a committed staff, dedicated parents, a supportive Board of Education and concerned community, the negative social statistics facing African American males can be reversed. While not every school can replicate our male-focused, African-Centered program, there are many schools with the concern and commitment to try some of the recommendations we have put forth here. We can save our sons—and in so doing, save our daughters too. Our moment is now—and it will take a nation of millions to hold us back.

NOTES

1. In 1957 in Little Rock, Arkansas, nine Black teenagers faced angry white mobs to integrate Central High School. The violence was so intense that then-President Dwight Eisenhower had to send combat troops from the 101st Airborne to halt the violence and protect these courageous young Black people.

2. The term "core texts" refers to primary, or basic, books used in various subject matter disciplines.

References

Adams, Debra. 1994. "Special Schools Do Fairly," *Detroit Free Press*. 20 June.

American Council on Education. 1988. *Minorities in Higher Education*. Seventh Annual Status Report. Washington, D.C.: Office of Minority Concerns.

Barashango, Ishakamusa. 1979. *Afrikan People and European Holidays: A Mental Genocide*. Silver Spring, MD: IVth Dynasty.

Bennett, Lerone. Jr. 1969. *Before the Mayflower: A History of Black America*. Chicago: Johnson Publishing Company.

Bond, Horace Mann. 1970. *The Education of the Negro in the American Social Order*. Third Edition. New York: Octagon Books, first published in 1934.

Center for the Study of Social Policy. 1984. *The Flip Side of Female-Headed Families: The Economic Status of Black Males*. Washington, D.C.

_____. 1993(a). *Keeping Pace With Change: Black Males and Social Policy*. Washington, D.C.

_____. 1993(b). *The Flip-Side of Black Female-Headed Families: Black Adult Men*. Washington, D.C.

Dawson, M.C. 1994. *Black Discontent: The Preliminary Report on the 1993-94 National Black Politics Study.* NBPS Report No. 1. April. Available from the author at the University of Chicago.

Detroit Public Schools. 1989. *Detroit Quality Education Plan.* Monographs (2) and (3).

_____. 1990. *Improving Self-Concept for At-Risk Black Students,With Emphasis on Saving the Black Male.* Report of the First Annual Conference (March 10). 1 June.

_____. 1991. *Male Academy, Grades K-8: Report of the Male Academy Task Force.*

Detroit City Council. 1991. *The Plight of the African American Male.* Executive Summary of a Legislative Hearing, sponsored by Councilman Gil Hill.

Detroit Free Press. 1993. "The Other Class of '93," 6 June.

DuBois, W.E.B. 1903. *Souls of Black Folk.* New York: Fawcett (1961 Edition).

_____. 1933. "The Field and Function of the Negro College," *The Education of Black People: Ten Critiques,* 1906-1960. Ed., Herbert Aptheker. Amherst: University of Massachusetts, 1973.

ERIC Clearinghouse on Urban Education, Institute for Urban and Minority Education. 1991. *School Programs for African American Male Students.* New York: Teachers College, Columbia University, May.

Fanon, Frantz. 1963. *The Wretched of the Earth*. New York: Grove.

Gibbs, Jewelle Taylor. 1988. *Young, Black, and Male in America: A Endangered Species*. New York: Auburn House.

Gundersen, Joan Rezner. 1986. "The Double Bonds of Race and Sex: Black and White Women in a Colonial Virginia Parish," *The Journal of Southern History*, LII (3), August.

Hamilton, Arthur, Jr. 1993. *Father Behind Bars*. Waco, Texas: WRS Publishing.

Henry, Charles P. *Jesse Jackson: The Search for Common Ground*. Oakland: Black Scholar Press, 1991.

Higginbotham, A. Leon, Jr. 1978. *In the Matter of Color: Race and the American Legal Process*. Volume One. New York: Oxford University Press.

Holland, Spencer. 1991. "Elementary and Secondary Education—Special Populations: Positive Role Models for Primary-Grade Black Inner-City Males," *Equity and Excellence*, 25, 1.

_____. 1993. *Keynote Presentation, Conference of National Council of African American Males*, Chicago, Illinois. August.

Hopkins, Ronnie. (1994) *Teaching Black Males "By Any Means Necessary!": Critical Lessons in Schooling,*

Community and Power. Ph.D. Dissertation. East Lansing: Michigan State University.

Horton, Carrell Peterson and Smith, Jessie Carney. 1990. *Statistical Record of Black America*. Detroit: Gale Research.

Huskisson, Gregory. 1988. "The Men at the Bottom," *Detroit Free Press,* December 18.

Jones, Rhett S. 1993. "Double Burdens, Double Responsibilities: Eighteenth-century Black Males and the African American Struggle," *African American Male Studies*. I (1), Winter. Pp. 1-14.

Lee, Carol D. 1992. "Profile of an Independent Black Institution: African-Centered Education at Work," *Journal of Negro Education*, LXI (2). Pp. 160-77.

Logan, Rayford W. and Winston, Michael R. 1982. *Dictionary of American Negro Biography*. New York: Norton. Pp. 422-424.

Madhubuti, Haki. 1990. *Black Men: Obsolete, Single, Dangerous? The Afrikan American Family in Transition*, Chicago: Third World Press.

Malcolm X Academy. 1991. *Quality Education*. Detroit: Public Schools.

Mauer, Marc. 1990. *Young Black Men and the Criminal Justice System: A Growing National Problem*. Washington, D.C.: The Sentencing Project.

_____. 1991. *Americans Behind Bars: A Comparison of International Rates of Incarceration.* Washington, D.C.: The Sentencing Project.

_____. 1992. *Americans Behind Bars: One Year Later.* Washington D.C.: The Sentencing Project.

McCall, Nathan. 1994. *Makes Me Wanna Holler: A Young Black Man in America.* New York: Random House.

McGriff, Deborah M. 1993. *Memo to Detroit School Board.* 30 September.

Mchawi, Basir. 1993. "Where is Ujamaa Institute?" *The City Sun*, (New York), October 6-12.

Milwaukee Public Schools. 1990. *Educating African American Males: A Dream Deferred.* Milwaukee Public School District, May.

Moore and Associates. 1994. *1992-93 African-Centered Academies Evaluation, Final Report.* July. Used with permission.

Moore, Debra. *The African Roots of Mathematics.*

National Urban League Research Department. 1990. *Quarterly Economic Report on the African-American Worker*, Report No. 23, Fourth Quarter 1989, Table 8. Washington, D.C.: National Urban League Inc., March.

_____. *Quarterly Economic Report on the African-American Worker.* 1992. Report No. 31, Fourth Quarter 1991, Table 11. Washington, D.C.: National Urban League, Inc., May.

_____. Forthcoming. *Quarterly Economic Report on the African-American Worker*, Report No. 34, First Quarter 1994. Washington, D.C.: National Urban League, Inc.

Nelson, Jill. 1991. "Racist or Realistic?," *USA Weekend.* 17-19 May.

New Orleans Public Schools. 1988. *Educating Black Male Youth: A Moral and Civic Imperative.* Report of the Committee to Study the Status of the Black Male in the New Orleans Public Schools.

O'Brien, Eileen M. 1989. "1988 ACE Annual Report Sounds the Alarm: Higher Ed Community Must Act on the Crisis of the Black Male," *Black Issues in Higher Education.* 19 January.

O'Neal, Shaquille. 1993. *Shaq Attaq!* New York: Hyperion.

Poinsett, Alex. 1988. "Young Black Males in Jeopardy: Risk Factors and Intervention Strategies." *Report of Meeting at Carnegie Foundation of New York.* February.

Portland Public Schools. 1987. *African American Baseline Essays.* Portland, Oregon: Public Schools.

Quarles, Benjamin. 1973. *The Negro in the American*

Revolution. New York: Norton.

Riordan, Cornelius H. 1990. *Girls and Boys in Schools: Together or Separate?* New York: Teachers College.

Russell, Ron. 1994. "Schools of Choice Get Bad Marks." *Detroit News.* 15 February.

Sanford, Terry (U.S. Senator), "Opening Statement," *The Plight of African-American Men in Urban America, Hearings Before the Committee on Banking, Housing, and Urban Affairs,* United States Senate, March 19, 1991. Washington, D.C.: U.S. Government Printing Office. Pp. 3-5.

Sanford, Terry. 1991. *Senate Committee Hearing.* March.

Sedler, Robert. 1991. *Memorandum of Opinion.* 7 May.

Shakus, Sanyika. 1993. *Monster.* New York: Atlantic Monthly.

Shammas, Carolyn. 1985. "Black Women's Work and the Evolution of Plantation Society in Virginia, " *Labor History,* XXVI.

Sklar, Holly. 1993. "Young and Guilty by Stereotype," Z. July/August.

Smitherman, Geneva. *Memoirs of a Daughter in the Hood.* Work-in-progress.

_____. Ed. 1981. *Black English and the Education of Black Children and Youth.* Detroit: Wayne State

University Center for Black Studies.

Soderman, Anne K. and Phillips, Marian. 1986. "The Early Education of Males: Where Are We Failing Them?" *Educational Leadership*. Pp. 70-72.

U.S. Department of Labor. 1989. *Handbook of Labor Statistics*, Bulletin 2340. August.

Walker, David. 1829, 1830. *Appeal, in Four Articles; Together With a Preamble, to the Coloured Citizens of the World, but in Particular, and Very Expressly, to Those of the United States of America.* Baltimore, Maryland: Black Classic Press, 1993 Edition.

Watson, Clifford. 1984. *Afro-American Pioneers in Science.*

Weathers, Diane. 1983. "Stop the Guns," *Essence.* December.

Wilson, Reginald. 1981. "Standardized Tests and Educational Inequality," *Black English and the Education of Black Children and Youth*, ed., Geneva Smitherman. Detroit: Wayne State University Center for Black Studies.

Woodson, Carter G. 1933. *Miseducation of the Negro.* Washington, D.C.: Associated Publishers.

Appendices

SAVING THE BLACK MALE CONFERENCE RESOLUTION

[Participants at the March 10 conference unanimously passed the resolution below. It is a charge specifically to Michigan's Governor, Detroit-area Representatives to the Michigan Legislature and the U.S. Congress, the Wayne Country Board of Commissioners, and the Detroit Board of Education.]

Wheras, there is a national crisis in the condition of African American males;

Whereas, they have made the least educational and economic progress of all groups over the past decade;

Whereas, homicide is the leading cause of death for African American males, ages 15-19;

Whereas, over half of African American males, ages 16-24 are unemployed;

Whereas, African American females outnumber African American males by as much as 10 to 1 in some age groups in urban areas;

Whereas, more African American males are expelled

and suspended from school than African American females and males from other racial groups; and;

Whereas, the condition of African American males is so severe that researchers have labeled them as an "endangered species";

Be it therefore resolved that we call upon the following federal, state and local elected officials to convene hearings on the crisis of the African American male:

John Conyers, Jr.; George W. Crockett, Jr,; Carl Levin; Donald W. Riegle, Jr.; James J. Blanchard; Floyd Clack; Charlie J. Harrison; David S. Holmes, Jr.; Morris W. Hood, Jr.; Teola Hunter; Carolyn Kilpatrick; Raymond Murphy; Nelson Saunders; Virgil C. Smith, Jr.; Alma Stallworth; Ethel Terrell; Jackie Vaughn III; Ted Wallace; Juanita Watkins; Joseph Young Jr.; Joseph Young Sr.; Kay Beard; Arthur Blackwell; Edward Boike; David Cavanagh; Jackie Currie; George Cushingberry; Susan Heintz; Susan Hubbard; Kevin Kelley; Bernard Kilpatrick; Milton Mack; William O'Neil; Ricardo A. Solomon; Alberta Tinsley-Williams; Clarence Young; Keith Butler; Clyde Cleveland; Gilbert Hill; Barbara-Rose Collins; David Eberhard; Nicholas Hood; Jack Kelley; Maryann Mahaffey; Mel Ravitz; Edna Bell; Joseph Blanding; Gloria C. Cobbin; Kay Everett; Frank Hayden; Josh Mack; David Olmstead; Rose Mary Osborne; Lawrence Patrick; Ben W. Washburn; Alexander C. Wright.

YOUNG LIVES NEED ADULT HELP TODAY

Susan Watson
Detroit Free Press **Columnist**

(Reprinted with permission of *Detroit Free Press* from
Monday, March 12, 1990)

When you get too big for your britches, it usually has
nothing to do with your weight.

Last week, I ripped my britches at the seam. Now it's
mending time.

A phone call came in around deadline. A young
woman said she had been told to call me about getting
publicity for a certain event. It was a perfectly ordinary call;
I get them all the time.

But for some reason, maybe because she called at a
bad time, I sat up straight in my chair, sharpened my claws
and informed that young woman that providing free
publicity was not my major job in life.

The only thing more sobering than the silence on the
other end of the line was the young woman's voice as she
excused herself from the conversation.

On Saturday, I apologized. I still think she considers
me an arrogant, self-seeking son of a. . . ahem. . . daughter
of a plumber. I can't say I blame her.

The young woman, 20-year old Chantille Bouldes, was
among a handful of Michigan State University students who
were promoting a Saturday conference entitled "Saving the
Black Male."

The session was pulled together by MSU Professor
Geneva Smitherman and school principals Joseph Gilbert of
Mackenzie High School and Clifford Watson of Woodward

Elementary School. The program was sponsored by Area B of the Detroit Public Schools.

About 400 people, including a large number of young black males showed up at Brooks Middle School for talks and workshops led by locally and nationally recognized educators and community leaders.

A couple of handouts explained the problems in terms of numbers: 610,000 black men between the ages of 20 and 29 are in jail or under the control of the criminal justice system, while only 436,000 black men of all ages are enrolled in college, more than half of the black males between the ages of 16 and 24 are unemployed in some cities; a working man is twice as likely to marry the mother of his children as an unemployed one.

I'll forget the exact numbers, I know I will. But I won't forget two events that pasted faces, including mine, on the statistics.

During an audience participation segment, a young Murray-Wright High School student who described himself as a member of P-BOT (Positive Brothers of Today) raised his hand. "The only people talking are older people," he said.

One after another, those young men said they needed help right now—today—in their struggle to survive. You'll lose another generation by the time you get started doing something," one youngster said impatiently. "If you're with us, c'mon: if you're not, bye," challenged another. The youngsters said they want teachers who can help them learn, not make them feel stupid, and they want textbooks that aren't written from a white viewpoint of the world.

They also said they need parents who believe in them and support them. They hurled their challenges on the wings of prayer.

About an hour after their presentation, Andrea

Williams, leader of the health workshop, offered the audience another challenge. She sailed it gently through the air so that each person could catch it if he wanted.

Williams, an assistant principal at Tappan Middle School, said that all of the participants in other groups decided to make an immediate change—if only a little one—in their lives. Each person agreed to start doing something that day to help solve the problems facing our children.

That "something" could be as simple as pulling a child away from the TV and giving her a book to read. It could involve tutoring at a local school, getting involved in a youth group or spending time with a young neighbor who needs to talk to someone.

The important thing, William explained, is that you do something today—not tomorrow or next week.

I know that Williams' suggestion won't solve the whole problem, but it certainly will cut down on the mending we'll have to do later on.

GROUPS INSTILL BLACK PRIDE IN SCHOOL
Saving young males the focus of conference

Denise Crittendon
Detroit News **Staff Writer**

(Reprinted with Permission of *Detroit News* from Sunday,
March 11, 1990)

One year ago, he was so frustrated he skipped school just to hang out on street corners, talking loud and acting "cool."

Today, he goes by "Scrooge," a nickname his friends gave him because he watches the stock market, keeps tabs on the Dow Jones average and has plans to become an accountant.

In the last 12 months, Scrooge has become a P-BOT—a Positive Brother of Today.

"We spread black awareness in the schools," he said of P-BOT, which is composed of male students at Murray-Wright High School. "We want an Afro-centric awareness in the schools so students will know who they are. How can a tree grow without its roots? It can't. If we can acquire that, we can go on to more positive things."

Scrooge, a senior, who spoke on condition he not be named, was among nearly 500 attending "Saving the Black Male," a conference sponsored by the Area B region of the Detroit Public Schools. Saturday's one-day conference at Brooks Middle School in Detroit attracted parents, students, educators and about 20 members of P-BOT.

Speakers included author Haki Madhubuti, publisher of Third World Press in Chicago and professor at Chicago State University; Edward Vaughn of Vaughn's Book Store; and Adam Shakor, deputy mayor of Detroit.

Dr. Clifford Watson, principal of Woodward Elementary, an Area B school, said the conference was an attempt to stem the growing problems among young black urban males.

He said young black males make up 40 percent of the nation's homicide victims, and are expelled from school at a disproportionate level. The group also represents 50 to 60 percent of the dropouts in urban schools.

A recent study released by the Sentencing Project, a non-profit group in Washington D.C. reported that one in four African-American males in their 20s have had some brush with the penal justice system.

"We're trying to come up with some solutions," Watson said. "We're holding programs like this to reach the parents and to try to reach these guys early."

Scrooge, who spoke briefly to the audience, said P-BOT was formed to instill pride in young black men. He said most of the guys in P-BOT are former problem students, like himself. His life changed, he said, the day he found out about Malcolm X, a black leader slain in the 60s.

"I felt, wow, this guy was pretty cool," he said. "I became curious and I started going to the library and reading about African dynasties and kings and queens, and I found out that the Garden of Eden was in East Africa.

"For the first time, I felt like somebody," he said. "Then I started wondering, why were they (the power structure) hiding this from us? Why are they afraid to let us know this?"

The other members of P-BOT were undergoing a similar transformation. "They are so excited by the change," Scrooge said, "they spend most of their time reading and talking about black history."

"If they (the students) all found this out, they'd be like us (P-BOT)—united," he said.

BLACK YOUTH: CHALLENGE AND
OPPORTUNITIES FOR THE 21ST CENTURY

Dr. Jewelle Taylor Gibbs
University of California Berkeley

[After detailing the crises of Black youth, especially males, Dr. Gibbs outlined a ten-point program for solving problems].

I think, in general, we need to restructure our educational system from top to bottom. It's not that it just doesn't work for Black people; it doesn't really work for anyone. We are producing a country of illiterate people. We are producing a country of high school seniors who cannot locate Canada and Mexico on the map. We are producing a country of high school seniors, white, black, yellow, and brown, who cannot do simple math. We are producing a group of high school seniors who don't know who the last three Presidents were in this country. How can we say our educational system is even competitive? We can't compete with Japan, West Germany, and many other industrial nations. So we really have to change our schools for everyone . . . We cannot afford to continue losing one out of every four Black males in this country to unemployment, to drugs, or to crime. We need to pressure our local governments, our local school boards to get funds, such as Head Start, and to put those funds into our community so that our children start off on the right foot ready to go to kindergarten, first grade and to have what we call, "reading readiness." So let's get out there and get all the funds for early childhood education.

Secondly, we need to have increased funding for all of the programs that used to be called "Compensatory

Education Program." If we have Headstart and then don't make sure that the children keep up the gains they've made, they will begin to fall back. So we need to make sure that our schools have all of the federal and state funding coming to them. We need to make sure that our school bureaucracy is efficient; get those grant requests in on time. We need to be sure that we are getting our slice of the pie for urban schools. We are talking about computers in the classroom, language training labs in the junior high and high schools, and modern science equipment. Look at the kind of equipment these suburban schools have and then come to some of our inner-city schools. In Oakland [California] there may be one computer in the library, and then they lock that at lunch so the kids can't even use it. We have to demand the kind of equipment that will prepare our students for an economy that is highly technological.

Third, we have to improve teacher recruitment and teacher training. Now I don't want to come and bash teachers. I know teachers have to solve problems that the rest of society has ignored. But what is happening to our teachers? By the year 2000, fewer than 5% of this nation's teachers will be Black. We need more Black teachers in our schools, and we need more good teachers, no matter what the color of their skin. We need to go to these universities, and we have to say, "What are you doing to teach teachers how to deal with minority students? What do you have in our curriculum to tell them that minority students may have some different styles of learning, may have some different needs. What are you teaching them about the cultures of the minority students?" If you get a teacher who's well prepared, coming into an inner-city classroom who doesn't know anything about Black history, or Black culture, or Black family formation, that teacher may not be able to communicate effectively with those students. We've got to get more minority teachers, and we've got to improve teacher training.

Fourth, we must have comprehensive service for African American children. I agree with the notion that the school does have to fulfill some of the responsibilities that families used to fulfill because we have so many broken families and so many dysfunctional families. We have so many young mothers on crack. We have so many neglected children. When they come to school, it may be the safest, cleanest, most orderly place in their lives. We have to take advantage of those few hours we have these children in schools every day. We have to have health services, counseling services and drug prevention programs in our schools. We must have job referrals for young men who are not going to college. And we need the concept of "lighted school house." When European immigrants came here many years ago, we had lighted school houses on the East Coast and in the Midwest; right here in Detroit, you had lighted school houses. They were open all evening, taught adult education, citizenship, health, parent education, etc. We not only have to have education for our children; we need education for their parents.

Fifth, we need to reorient the priorities of our young Black males and reward them for academic excellence, not just athletic excellence. Of course, athletics is important, and of course, we all approve and are always happy to see a young man or a young woman with athletic prowess, but we also have to be realistic. Colleges recruit the athletes. They exploit our athletes, but they do not graduate our athletes, and when the glory days are over, they are out looking for short-order cook jobs, dishwashing jobs and low-income menial jobs because they have not got a college degree. We have to do in junior high and high school the same things for our good students that we do for our athletes. Our honor students should have varsity sweaters, and they should have a recognition banquet every year. Our honor students should be the ones who wear the pins and get the trophies. Let's start on Monday in our schools in Detroit, people from the City Council, and the Board of Education, let's put in a system of reward for our good students. Let's give them a City-wide day. Let's make them stars!

I just want to give you a personal story. I'm a preacher's daughter; and maybe some of you have already guessed that from my preaching style. My father died in 1981, and he had devoted his life to educating the young Blacks in our community and also his six children. A year after his death, we realized that the most important things that we could do to carry on his memory was to set up a scholarship in his name. That scholarship is now nine years old. It's called the Taylor Scholarship Fund. We started off giving $500 to the highest graduating Black senior. The scholarship has grown now in nine years, and the entire community now supports it. We now give one scholarship for $1,000 to the highest Black high school graduate and a scholarship to the highest ranking Black student in each elementary school through the sixth grade. At the banquet last summer, each of them got $100 and a number of prizes donated by local businesses. We honored 20 Black students of high academic achievement with their parents, their friends, and their teachers in the audience. We have seen in just nine years how rewarding academic excellence has turned around the Black students in our small town. Now they want to come to that banquet, and they want to get that money, and they want to get those prizes. This is what we need to do with every community in this country.

Sixth, we need comprehensive health clinics in schools. Many of the self-destructive behaviors that children engage in are due to lack of knowledge, support and early intervention. We need health clinics with trained nurses, doctors, and counselors who can spot the children on drugs, spot those who may be sexually active, spot the little girls who are getting pregnant early, and try to intervene at a very early stage. These clinics need services, including family planning. We have got to stop the epidemic of teenage pregnancy in our communities...

Seventh, we need to reorganize our schools to meet the developmental needs of our children. The Carnegie Foundation, about a year ago, issued a wonderful report entitled, "Turning Point," about how we need to reorganize middle and junior high schools in this country. Our Black males have certain developmental needs. Just like all children, they need caring teachers, small classrooms, creative learning environments, opportunities for service to the community and positive social experiences. Most of all, our teachers need to demonstrate to our children, male and female, alike, the expectation that they can achieve. I believe teachers should be accountable for students' learning. When we go to a doctor, and the doctor doesn't diagnose our illness, the doctor is the one held accountable. When we go to a lawyer, and the lawyer doesn't win our case, the lawyer is held accountable. When children do not learn to read and write, normal children—all of whom should be able to read and write, when they do not learn to read and write, I think we have to hold our teachers accountable.

Before, the parents all clapped; now the teachers have their turn. My eighth point is for parents. We need to involve parents in the educational mission. That's why I'm glad to see so many parents here today with their children. Dr. James Comer has a very wonderful program in New Haven, Connecticut where parents work with teachers and staff to create more effective schools for the children. When children see their parents involved in school, that gives a message to the child that school is important. That gives a message to the child that you are going to work with their teacher, not against their teacher. Don't just go down to the school when you get mad with the teacher. A parent will show up if you give Johnny a little whip on his backside, or if you punish Johnny, or if you look the wrong way at Judy. Mothers will be down there on Mondays: what did you do to my child? Well, I'll tell you, we need to go there sometimes to say good things to the teacher. We need to use our skill and our time. That means grandparents too and other retired people. Come into the schools. Give them your time and service.

Ninth, schools need to develop closer ties with local businesses, churches, civic organizations, professional groups, and labor unions so that everybody supports the educational mission. We're all in this together, and we need to have professional Black men and women come into the schools and show what they have done with their lives, to show what it means to be successful, to show that you can make it if you work hard enough, that you don't have to sell drugs to have a little money or to have a nice home. So we need to bring everybody into this common effort.

My tenth and final point is that education is part of a larger political process. Teachers, administrators and parents must make their voices heard at every level of the political process. Through your professional organizations, individually and as voters, bring pressure on your local school board, state legislature, and federal government to fund educational programs at levels which will provide good education for our students. We must say to our government: we come first. We're American taxpayers. Help us before you go to Nicaragua, Czechoslovakia, Romania, East Germany, the Philippines, Vietnam, etc.

BLACK MEN: OBSOLETE, SINGLE, DANGEROUS? THE AFRICAN AMERICAN FAMILY IN TRANSITION

Haki Madhubuti, Publisher
Third World Press, Chicago

[Using the title of his published book as springboard, Mr. Madhubuti challenged the audience to rethink and redefine their purpose in life in order to save Black youth. Excerpts from his speech are printed below].

Act with definition or need. The Ethiopians have a saying: a cat may go to a monastery, but she still remains a cat. Knowing one's self is key to knowing and understanding others. If a person hides from this thing of self now, his or her life will be built upon a bed of quicksand; from that comes slow but certain confusion, pain, self-doubt, and lonely death. All people need to take charge of their lives. The more a person understands her or his mind and body, the less she or he will destroy it. Ignorance breeds weakness and fear; one's history and culture are important to good life. If you don't know who you are, you'll be forever fighting other people's wars. All people need to ask the simple and correct questions that define life: 1) Why am I here? 2) Are we here to serve others or ourselves? Remember the proverb: wood may remain 10 years in the water, but it will never become a crocodile. Find the reason for your own existence and condition. Respect learning. Seek to be world class in everything that you do. The best way to do this is through study, work, more study and more work....

Black boys, Black girls and others need possibilities.

They need to know that there is a better tomorrow for them. This means that they need to be around successful and caring mothers and fathers, aunts and uncles, grandparents, and all the alternatives that are in the family and then those alternatives who are outside that nuclear extended family who are simply doing positive things in this world. So we need to have a better grasp of what success is....

At our school in Chicago, we graduate children who are at least two years ahead when they come out. There's no secret; the key is, parents and teachers have got to work like a family. Going to school is just like going to another home; that's the way it should be. What I mean to say is that children cannot function in our schools unless their parents are intimately involved with the school. The teaching that goes on in the schools carries on into the home. You have to realize that receiving a quality education is not only for you, to get you a star, but to make your overall life better. Education has got to be put into a much more wholistic paradigm if we agree that things we work for are worth it.

The next level that we have to think about is taking these schools, as well as our cultural institutions, initially what we call the African American Cultural Boot Camp. I'm saying that we must become involved in parenting. Men must form men's groups that aid in developing these young brothers. Due to lack of functioning families, we must, in the meantime, develop alternatives. Year-round boys and girls camps. Let's not talk about the kind of boot camp that these white people are talking about. I'm saying an African American Cultural Boot Camp. I'm working with some men on the national level trying to begin initiating this. We're going to take young men and women for a week. Take them out of their setting, put them into a setting that is totally themselves, culturally, enriched; culturally put them at a level where, from 5:00 in the morning till 11:00 at night we've got them doing things that not only tell them about themselves but make them understand the world and their contributions to the world, but most importantly raising their self-esteem and telling them and teaching them that they are indeed important. Take them away from all the temptations of fate, sitting in front of a television set. There will be no television set. We have got to isolate, demand, BOOM-shock them into a new reality. But it won't work unless this reality is continuing in the community when we come back. Therefore, these African American Boot Camps have to be set up in our own institutions, wherever they may be.

Essentially, we have to become critical thinkers. Very seldom are people taught thinking skills. Early in childhood, we are told to use our minds and how to use them; so therefore we are often more prone to believe than to think. It's much easier to believe challenges, competition, instruction, and study. Thinking often demands that a person be curious about the world, people, animals, vegetation, art....

Discipline and motivation. We've got to have discipline. One of the most disciplined things that we have to work on is the deterioration of the family. Anytime you see people not functioning, you can look back, and it will generally be the family. When you look at the one key element that any truly liberated people cannot do without, it's the family. That means that men and women must decide to get married later, and that they must be very conscious of how their children come into the world. The point is, when men and women make the decision to marry or to mate, that decision at some point has got to be based upon quality and intelligence. Just because she looks good, that's not good enough reason to marry her. I'm saying that once that decision is made and once the people begin to mate, then the dye is set. Once you get children, then it

126

seems to me at some point we understand what parenting is really about. It's not raising children up; it's about rearing children. It's about setting high goals and high thinking. These high goals and high thinking have got to be incorporated into the parents' lives also. Your children are exact mirrors of you, in many cases. It becomes key to say, "Okay, we're married, we have children." That means for 18, 19, years, you got to stay together. As long as the family is not being battered, as long as verbal abuse doesn't exist, you've got to stay together to make sure that the mother and father are there, to make sure that these children come up in an atmosphere that essentially leads them to a better understanding of tomorrow. The family is key.

There's got to be a change. We've got to be more self-reliant. America was built on the backs of our people. The greatness of the country was made possible, not only because of that, but because of small businesses. The multi-national corporations are recent phenomena. Small business, small cultural institutions are needed, those things that people turn to every day. Now in this year, 1990, there are approximately 15 million small businesses in America that may be family-owned. Small businesses are the major employers in the country, other than government. Recognize that we have got to reach our children early on, that they have got to move towards business, entrepreneurship. We got all these M.B.A.'s coming out, all these young undergraduates in business school, and they come out and want to work for the multi-national corporations, rather than come back and try to transform our communities. What we see in our communities are all other cultures opening up businesses. I think that if Arabs can make it in our communities, if a Korean can make it in our communities, then why can't we make it? We have got to teach these children early, because when they get to the

University of Michigan or Michigan State, there's a whole value and cultural thing that's going to change. They're being taught, essentially, to go for McDonald's rather than come back and try to change their communities....

The world is different from what it was 50 or 60 years ago. The person needs not only to be able to adapt to change, but he or she must be able to see change coming and initiate change. If you understand history, you understand how the economic system has changed over the last hundred years. It has grown from an agrarian base, to an industrial-based economy to what is becoming an economy based upon services and information gathering. Being computer-literate is important, but at the same time, you got to be able to read what is going on around the world in the areas of race, economic power, environment, and so forth.

I'm going to close off with *Black Men: Obsolete, Single, Dangerous?*...I put 12 years in this book. What I was concerned about is that the answers have to be in a cultural context. All people in this country, for the most part, control their own cultural inheritance. Show me a Polish person in Chicago...show me a Jewish person in Detroit...show me an Italian person in New York. I'm saying, these people think about themselves first; then they think about everybody else. We want to take on everybody else's problems, except our own, first and foremost. We must become number one, single-minded about our development and about our existence. There is a need for a new definition and new thinking—world class thinking...

∾